# Individualizing
# Your Reading Program

# The Putnam Series in Education

## A Publishing Program Dedicated to
## Education as a Profession: Assessment and Planning

Consulting Editors

### OLE SAND and ELAINE COOK
Wayne State University

---

# Individualizing
# Your Reading Program

## SELF-SELECTION IN ACTION

### Jeannette Veatch

Associate Professor
College of Education
Pennsylvania State University

**NEW YORK**  G. P. Putnam's Sons

# Contents

v

## APPENDIX

*Illustrations will be found following page 50.*

# Foreword

LEARNING TO READ is a virtual necessity for the American child. His parents expect him to learn to read; so do his teachers, relatives, and neighbors. In fact the whole community presumes that, if the school is doing its job well, the children of the locality will read efficiently and effectually.

Teaching the child to read is accepted by the school as one of its major responsibilities. Today's teachers assume that they must guide children in such ways that "little black marks" laid out neatly, linearly on pages of paper become meaningful signs, signals, and symbols. Educators continuously seek improved ways of developing in children a multi-faceted literacy. They know that a reader is one who does read for enjoyment, for information, for work-a-day pursuits, for being a good member of his community and his world.

As knowledge about learning theory, about child growth and development, about linguistics and communication arts, about the reading act itself has increased, the methods, procedures, and practices through which children are led to fathom the mysteries of the "little black marks" have changed or been refined. In the interest of the child and the culture— that the young may become the best readers it is possible for them to be—applications of what is salient and pertinent knowledge from such fields as psychology, child study, sociology, philosophy, and linguistics must be translated into educational theory and practice. New ways of teaching reading must be experimented with soundly and introduced into classrooms perceptively and dynamically. The individualizing of reading finds its bearings and garners its support from research findings that its proponents believe to be foundational in helping children toward proficiency in reading skills and abilities, as Dr. Jeannette Veatch points out in this book.

Individualizing reading practices is an attempt on the part of the teacher so to manage the classroom that each child is learning to read at his own "growing edges." Respect for the unique individuality of the child is safeguarded. The child purposes and plans and is thus intimately involved in establishing the thresholds of his own learnings. Instruction is paced to the individual's needs, concerns, lacks, aspirations. The selection of reading materials and resources is a matter of a particular child's recognition that "This is what I really want to try to read."

The individualizing of reading practices has already attracted a large number of perceptive, creative teachers who are seeking ways of making the reading act more pointedly meaningful for every child they teach. Other teachers, not quite so venturesome, want to learn more about this promising practice. This book by Dr. Veatch should be helpful both to teachers who are already involved in individualizing reading and to those who want to introduce more flexible procedures into highly structured and formalized reading programs.

Dr. Veatch respects teachers and their efforts to improve their teaching practices. As this book so clearly conveys, she wants children to know the thrilling satisfaction of learning to read with teachers who face the challenge of today's teaching with zest, imagination, and resourcefulness.

LELAND B. JACOBS
Teachers College, Columbia University

# Preface

IN SPITE of some confusion as to its meaning, the term "individualized reading" (or "individualizing reading") has come to indicate a special way of teaching in the classroom. Unfortunately, while the term clearly emphasizes the quality of individual instruction unique to this practice, it also seems to imply that grouping never occurs. This, of course, is not the case, as there is extraordinary opportunity for wise and efficient grouping in such a program.

Another widely used term is that of "self-selection." Yet it, too, is inadequate in its seeming denial of the *instructional* role of the teacher. Let no one think that this book deals with other than the major reading program in a classroom. The approach discussed in this book is not subordinate to or an adjunct of the common basal reading program—what we are considering here *is* the basic instructional program.

As such it has certain prime characteristics that occur regardless of the variations in practice found throughout the country. These are: 1) self-selection of material by pupils for their own instruction, 2) individual conferences between each pupil and teacher, and 3) groups organized for *other* than reasons of ability or proficiency in reading.

Many teachers confuse an individualized approach and recreational reading because both entail self-selection of books.

The difference lies in the *instructional* role of the teacher. For example, in recreational reading, we find the following:

A weekly or biweekly period
Little or no actual instruction
Teacher largely free and inactive once books are chosen
Little attention to skill development
Reading entirely silent

A quite different picture is found in the individualized approach, to wit:

A daily reading period
Continual instruction
Teacher active and in demand
Concern for skill development
Reading silent with frequent opportunities to read orally to the teacher and to the class

The area in which an individualized program makes its greatest contribution to reading instruction is that of classroom management. The concepts of seeking, self selection, and pacing lend a new element to the reading period. Some feel that the instruction with which this book deals does not represent a program at all, but is, rather, distinctly a teaching practice. This writer, however, believes that this is cutting semantics rather fine, and will use the concepts of program and practice interchangeably throughout the text.

As our emphasis will rest most heavily on the ways of managing a classroom during a reading period, the specifics of the reading act itself will be left to other sources. A child's energy and power when he is reading on a self-selection basis enormously reduces the need for a teacher to drill in phonics, word attack skills, the use of context and picture clues, and the like. Individualization gives a unique and unprecedented quality to the motivation which is the source of its strength. This is why this book is primarily concerned with the development of the *sequence of motivation*. While mechanics of reading are implicit in the body of the discussion, they will not be singled out for special treatment. The act and nature of reading, so well described in so many texts, is little different whether a child reads individually to his teacher or in a group to his class. However, the manner in which he approaches books, the way he chooses what he reads, his attitude toward instruction, what he does to help himself, and how he reacts to all the matters of motivation, success, and failure in reading are quite different under an individualized program than under any other. It is these areas of difference with which we will be concerned.

The text is divided into two parts. Part I describes, explains and supports an individualized reading program. It is designed to be particularly helpful to classroom teachers and their supervisors and principals in changing over from an ability-grouped program with basal or co-basal texts.

Part II is a collection of selected articles, largely examples of individualized reading in action, which were hitherto available only in scattered sources. Bringing them together in a single source will give aficionados of this departure from traditional reading practice easy access to important and valuable information.

It is hoped, too, that wider circulation of these excellent articles will spark further research. After all, it has only been nine years since individualized reading first received national recognition; consequently, there has been little time to develop a literature based on extensive research. Much remains to be done, and much is being done. This writer is particularly impressed with the survey of the experimentation in New York City public schools. It is currently available only in mimeographed form, but its impending publication for distribution on a wide basis will indeed make a contribution to the literature of individualized reading.

The development of individualized reading since its national recognition in 1952 has been nothing short of amazing. Educators everywhere have come to find an unsuspected community of interest in the matter, an interest which is being fed by a growing criticism of the traditional approach with its formalized ability-groups and omnipresent basal texts. This book has a point of view about reading which is presented individually by the present writer and collectively by the many authors represented in Part II. It is sincerely hoped that it will contribute to the further development of individualized reading programs so that teachers and children may be better served and that love of books may one day become the dominant feature of all reading instruction.

One educator reported that a budding teacher returned from his first observational experience and said, "Arithmetic teaching has changed. Music and art has changed. But the teacher I was with was teaching reading just the same way I was taught—a general assignment, three groups, hectograph sheets after each group. . . . Haven't we learned any NEW thing about teaching reading?"

We have indeed. It is a pattern which fits a reading program to the exact needs of pupils. It individualizes reading.

# Acknowledgments

MANY PEOPLE throughout the years have helped me shape the ideas expressed in this book. Their suggestions, encouragement, and support have been greatly appreciated. Although I am indebted to all of them, there are some to whom I would like to express special thanks:

To Dr. Alvina T. Burrows for her help when I was first trying to clarify my thinking about the teaching of reading.

To Mrs. Mary Bulcken and Mrs. Elizabeth Young of Baltimore, Maryland, whose work with children was an inspiration to watch and in whose classrooms I received more help than any amount of arm-chair thinking might have produced.

To Dr. Philip Acinapuro, who will make a name for himself with his own study and whose assistance as friend and editor greatly aided in the completion of my manuscript.

To Principal Mortimer J. Abramowitz and the faculty of Public School 167, Brooklyn, New York, for their kindness in allowing me to use photographs in their possession to illustrate this book.

To June McLeod, whose friendship and continuing encouragement never deterred her from wielding a drastic editorial pencil when she felt my manuscript was straying from the practical aspect of helping teachers.

And to my father, who throughout his life taught me that the *status quo* exists only to be questioned by folks like us.

xiii

# Part I

DESCRIPTION, DIRECTIONS,
AND PHILOSOPHY

| Chapter | WHY INDIVIDUALIZE |
|---|---|
| **1.** | READING? |

IN A DEMOCRACY we believe that each human being is unique and should have the opportunity to develop to his highest potential. It goes without saying that a democratic society must have a democratic school curriculum. Surely American schools have trouble enough providing adequate educational opportunity because of insufficient financial support without borrowing more problems through lack of progress in educational methodology.[1]

Years ago teachers began separating children into groups or classes of low, medium, or high ability. This was the most effective method of teaching known at the time. However, is the democratic ideal of equal opportunity for all to develop their talents fully best promoted by ability grouping? This writer thinks not. In the teaching of reading, at least, a methodology has been developed which enables teachers to provide full opportunity for each pupil without using ability grouping.

The process of self-selection of reading matter makes arbitrary separation of children into ability groups unnecessary. The democratic ideal of the uniqueness of the individual and of equal opportunity for growth is provided for. Individual

---

[1] Much of the thinking in this chapter is based on concepts and ideas originally presented in *Education Trend #654,* J. Veatch, "Individualized Reading—For Success in the Classroom," Arthur C. Croft Publications, New London, Connecticut, 1954.

interests and purposes can be realized and abilities can be developed as rapidly or as slowly as inherent growth potential makes possible. The practice of individualizing reading, through the concepts of seeking, self-selection, and pacing, meets the criteria of the democratic ideal. Furthermore, it provides an efficient method for meeting the wide range of differences which are common in any classroom group.

## Attempts to Meet Individual Differences

Since the very beginning, there have been attempts to meet the different needs of individual pupils. The history of education is full of teachers who endeavored to speed up slow learners or give special attention to fast learners. The dunce cap and the birch rod—however mistaken in their use—were indications that teachers recognized individual pupil differences. Any teacher *knows* that some children learn quickly while others do not, even though they might do little about it.

Education in our early days lumped large numbers of children together regardless of age or ability. Books were scarce and most children did not stay in school very long, if they attended at all. But the nation's population increased rapidly and democratic forces began to insist upon education for all as a public responsibility. All over the country, school authorities struggled with new problems, and the problem of individual differences was high on their list.[2] Out of the many attempts to cope with the variations in abilities of pupils, two major practices emerged: grade classification of pupils, and ability grouping within grades or schools.

At first the graded system separated children according to their ability to read particular books or accomplish certain

[2] See Gertrude Hildreth, "Individual Differences," *Encyclopedia of Educational Research*, p. 567, New York, Macmillan, 1950; H. J. Otto, "Organization and Administration," *Elementary Education*, III.

other academic tasks, but, by 1860, chronological age had become the major basis of grade organization. Children proceeded through their schooling on a yearly plan. But still more flexibility was needed to meet the different rates of learning. Ability grouping was the next development. It was based on the theory that children learn more readily when they are separated into whole classes, or groups within a class, on the basis of similar ability or achievement.

Yet in spite of the popularity of these two important forward steps, the search for better ways to meet individual differences has not stopped. Controversy and experimentation have continued. And although graded schools and ability grouping have never given full satisfaction, other plans, schemes, and panaceas for effectively coping with differences have never seemed to catch fire.

Teachers know, of course, that the best way to meet individual differences is to teach each child individually. Yet methods of doing just that have hitherto been based upon a concept of teacher assignment, or pupil contract, and have been so complicated that the great majority of teachers simply balk at using them—and not without reason. Many teachers have tried to manage their classrooms in some kind of an individual way. Frequently, however, either the classrooms have fallen into chaos, or the teachers have been forced to work unconscionable hours preparing and correcting individual work assignments. The pressure of large classes or extensive preparations (in addition to inadequate training in classroom management) has stifled much of the movement toward individualization; and rare indeed is the person who has been able to operate his classroom successfully on an individual basis.

But now the concept of pupil *self*-assignment as a solution to the problem of meeting individual differences has become a new element in the situation. For the first time we have a system whereby teachers do not need to prepare and correct a lesson for every activity of their pupils. Children may now be given an unprecedented degree of freedom to pursue their own interests and still receive adequate teacher guidance and help. Certainly in reading, on the evidence already available, teachers find that this pattern is practical and effective. In individualizing reading by using free choice of material, we have at last a way of keying learning more closely to the specific levels of each pupil. Self-selection represents a major breakthrough in the long search for better ways to meet individual differences.

## All Are Different

That no two children grow alike is a fact, provable and proven.[3] Everyone knows that children have two eyes, two ears, hair, and can be of the same age. Yet for learning purposes, 35 children in any classroom are 35 *different* persons, no matter how they are measured. Intelligence, height, weight, muscular coordination, and behavior traits all reveal a wide range of differences. Even in matters of energy and effort there is no such thing as uniformity. As Marie Hughes has pointed out, there is a rhythm of effort and relaxation in every individual.[4] The rhythms can never be the same in any two people. We grow and improve by leaps and spurts. We surge forward and then wait to catch our breath on a plateau. Our plateaus cannot coincide. Our surges cannot coincide.

Homogeneous grouping as a method of organizing a classroom is grossly inadequate if the problems arising from indi-

---

[3] See N. Bagley, and H. S. Conrad, "Child Development: General Aspects." *Encyclopedia of Educational Research,* New York, Macmillan, 1950, p. 141.

[4] "Theoretical Considerations Underlying Program of Self-Selection with Recommendations." In Delores C. Palmer, *To Determine the Reactions of 4th Graders to a Program of Self-Selection,* University of Utah, 1946 (Master's Thesis). Chapter VI by Marie Hughes.

vidual differences are to be met. Alice V. Keliher's critical evaluation of homogeneous grouping is one of the classic studies of educational literature.[5] Her arguments against the efficacy of homogeneous grouping have yet to be seriously challenged.

*Seldom are two children ready to be taught reading from the same material at the same time.* They should have a chance to seek and explore, to select and use the books and other materials most suited to their needs. It is doubtful that any one book can serve the common purpose of even *two* children for more than a day or two. Giving identical lessons to unlike children is a violation of natural development. No reading program can be truly successful unless it is easily adjustable to the enormous variety of growth patterns, purposes, and interests found in any class. (See page 23.)

Children *can* be grouped homogeneously on the basis of *one* specific skill, or *part* of a skill, or a *definitely isolated* deficiency or interest for the period of time necessary to improve upon the skill or interest or to ameliorate the deficiency. This is functional grouping for a clearly defined purpose.

## Seeking, Self-selection, and Pacing

The traits of seeking, self-selection, and pacing are inborn characteristics of man and animals. When creatures explore their surroundings they exhibit seeking behavior. When they take something from that environment to promote their own growth, they show the process of self-selection. When they use whatever has been selected, they pace the consumption at the proper rate for their own development. Examples of these traits can be cited at any level of the animal world.

In an individualized reading program seeking, self-selection

[5] *Critical Evaluation of Homogeneous Grouping,* Bureau of Publications, Columbia University Teachers College, 1931.

and pacing also come into play. For example, children use seeking behavior to explore the classroom or library book supply. They will select, if the supply is sufficient, a book that is right for their reading development at that time. Further, children will read those selected books at the pace that is most suitable to their needs. If allowed to operate, these traits can become valuable adjuncts to teaching.

Indeed, seeking, self-selection, and pacing *are* the motivations which spur children on in an individualized reading program. Their existence as natural traits guarantees a source of energy and power which activates children to work and work hard, with joy and with satisfaction. They are not merely useful for learning, they are absolutely necessary.[6]

## Goals and Questions in Reading Instruction

There is no disagreement among educators about the kind of reading we would like to see developed in children. Everyone would concur on goals such as the following:

1. All children should be able to read at the peak of their ability.
2. All children should know what it is like to enjoy the world of books.
3. All children should be able to read to find out the facts that they need to know.
4. All children should be able to read aloud well enough to give pleasure to listeners.
5. All children should be able to sort out fact from fiction in their reading.
6. All children should be able to develop their own philosophy of living from books as well as from other sources.

[6] Also note thinking of Willard Olson and May Lazar, in this volume.

No educator, short of insanity, would agree that it is good for children to:

1. Hate books and avoid reading them whenever possible.
2. Be ashamed to read aloud in front of others.
3. Dread the periods when the teacher teaches reading.
4. Deliberately avoid planning to enter a vocation that requires reading.
5. Develop a philosophy of living without consideration of ideas found in writings and books.

The end product of reading instruction, without question, should be a child who loves reading, who seeks reading, and who benefits from it.

Yet even though educators' goals may be the same, there is deep and profound controversy about ways in which they may be reached.

For example:

1. Is ability grouping the best way in which reading instruction can be organized?
2. Are basic series and their teacher's guides the best tools for teaching reading?
3. Are trade books more or less important than basal readers in an instructional reading program, or are they equally so?
4. Is rigidly controlled vocabulary more important than interesting material?
5. Are we sure that what we *try* to teach through carefully worked out lesson plans is *actually* what children learn?
6. Can children wisely choose their own material for reading instruction?

These are but a few of the questions about which teachers of reading disagree.

## Comparing Two Programs

The chart on pages 12-13 lists some of the salient techniques and principles of individualized and of ability-grouped reading programs. Of course some teachers might vary a basal reading program with a practice which is cited under the heading of individualized reading. Similarly, other teachers who have individualized their reading program might use an idea listed under the heading of ability-grouped reading.

As can be seen, these two methods are sharply divergent on matters of book selection, grouping practices, lesson planning, and teacher-pupil interaction. While some teachers may shift from one program to another at times, the basic philosophies of individualized and of ability-grouped reading differ profoundly.

The conditions of self-selection, individual conferences, and short-term grouping must be operative in an individual reading program as here presented. They do not all need to occur at the same time and to the same extent. But regardless of the degree of emphasis by a given teacher, it is the extent to which these conditions exist which determines the extent to which an individualized program exists.

Individualized reading, with its unique contribution of self-selection, is a new concept on the educational horizon. Ability-grouping and basal texts are decades old. We know that children are reading better than they ever did, but are they reading as well as they should? (More than one voice has suggested that schools should be doing better than that!) Are they improving as much as they could? If there has been too little progress, ability grouping and basal readers must not be ignored as causes, for ability grouping and the use of basal readers have dominated reading practice in this country for years.

Recently there have been healthy signs of loosening of lock-step methods in reading. Many basal series are increasingly advocating measures such as the use of more than one text and extensive free reading, and the reading problem is infinitely worsened if administrators and teachers fail to respond to those minimal recommendations of a basal program. But even the most enlightened and flexible basal reader program can be criticized for its omission of self-selection and independent reading as a core.

Although reading achievement is improving in this country, it is not improving enough: and the blame for this too meagre growth rests on those who, perhaps knowing no better, have led children to read books and other materials which are remote from their purpose. A new and different method of teaching reading is needed to replace the outmoded basic reader programs now in vogue in American schools.

Returning to the chart, let us use the comparisons set forth there in single sentence form to structure a fuller discussion of individualized reading vis-à-vis ability-grouped reading.

## I Reading Materials

### A. Large Number and Variety of Trade and Textbooks Used in Instruction

Perhaps the clearest evidence of the ferment occurring in the field of reading is the increase in use of trade books in schools —that is, books designed for the general bookstore and library market rather than for text use. Many educators have long asked the question, "Why can't these wonderful books be used in *learning* to read?" Indeed, they can.

Using fine books in a school program offers no difficulty if they are available in sufficient quantity and are somewhere near the class reading level in difficulty. Their appeal is such that

INDIVIDUALIZED READING          ABILITY-GROUPED READING

### I  Reading Material

A. Large number and variety of trade and textbooks used in instruction ↔ A. Single basic or supplemental readers used in instruction

### II  Classroom Organization and Procedure

A. Children choose what they read ↔ A. Teacher chooses what children read

B. Motivation arises from child's interests ↔ B. Motivation comes from teacher using the manual

C. Instruction on individual one-to-one basis ↔ C. Instruction on group basis

D. Grouping is short term and for specific, immediate purpose ↔ D. Grouping is semi-permanent and for indeterminate purpose

E. Reading lesson prepared independently and seatwork has element of self-determination ↔ E. Reading lesson prepared in a group and seatwork determined by teacher

F. Remedial work integrated with other activities ↔ F. Remedial work entails separate operation

G. Planned sharing period ↔ G. No special sharing period

H. Individual peak reading level checked and evaluated ↔ H. Various and indeterminate reading levels checked and evaluated

## III  *Effects on the Child and on His Reading*

A. Gifted child progresses at his own pace  ↔  A. Gifted child must gear progress to group's

B. Slow reader not publicly stigmatized  ↔  B. Slow reader publicly stigmatized by group and book assignment

C. Close personal interaction with teacher  ↔  C. Child loses advantage of close personal interaction with teacher

D. Reading at own interest and ability level fosters development of skills  ↔  D. Working at group interest and ability level may hinder development of skills

E. Acquiring skills only as needed assures their normal development  ↔  E. Acquiring skills when not needed may hinder reading competence

F. Oral reading promoted by genuine audience situation  ↔  F. Oral reading suffers through absence of genuine audience situation

G. Reading becomes its own reward  ↔  G. Extrinsic rewards may debase intrinsic value of reading

children prefer them. Even comic books will come off second best in competition with good trade books.

The real reason for learning to read is enjoyment and personal satisfaction. When children choose a book, they should do so because they will enjoy reading it. If there are trade books that they like, why should they not read them? If there is nothing "good" to read, is reading worth the effort? When books of all kinds are available, children can make a genuine choice. Books with the greatest interest appeal will be the most read.

There are other reasons why exposure to many kinds of books do more than just promote reading. Such an ingathering exposes children to the works of creative artists and writers. The riches of the world are at their command. Values and tastes are enriched. The use of self-selection in the teaching of reading can acquaint children with the classics of literature in addition to its other benefits. When teachers are not required to demand reading from basal texts, they are free to encourage the exploration of other kinds of books. When a great variety of books are available, many will be read for their own sake— *not* because a teacher has made them required reading.

If our goal is to help the child love to read and to seek reading for its own sake, surely the riches of the literary world, the best in artistic make-up, in creative writing, and, of course, in reader appeal is an inestimable help toward reaching this goal. But even aside from the fact that strict reliance upon basal readers is inadequate if we are to reach this goal, there are serious questions to be asked about basal readers *per se*.

1. *Should basal readers be used basically?* Teachers' manuals for basic series and all texts on the teaching of reading talk about provision for meeting individual needs. But in actual practice, teachers gear instruction to *group* needs because that is the way the reading program is structured. Attention to indi-

vidual needs under a basal system too often receives but lip service. Busy teachers are hard pressed to give it more.

Even Russell,[7] a proponent and author of basic readers and texts on the teaching of reading, cites these dangers:

"1. The children of any one class cannot all profit by the same book of a basic series.

2. A basic series of readers cannot capitalize upon the community environment of a particular school or the interesting news events (local, national, international) which occur every week.

3. A basic series of readers should not be used to make reading something apart from the rest of the school program.

4. A basic series of readers may not provide all the reading situations needed by some children."

An analysis of these four dangers of basic readers must logically raise the question of why they should be used *basically* at all? Why should such books (or *any* books, for that matter) be assigned to children en masse? Are the advantages really great enough to offset the disadvantages?

This is not to say that there are not some books in basal series which are helpful, useful, and suitable. But it is meant to question the *basal* use of basal readers.

2. *Do basal readers lack appeal?* In the primary grades the answer to this question is "Yes." James L. Hymes [8] points out that in spite of notable improvement in format, in vocabulary control, and the like, basal readers fail on the matter of appeal, which is the main reason for reading in the first place. Would children choose these books if they had freedom of choice? John Hersey calls primers "pallid" because of their

---

[7] D. A. Russell, *Children Learn to Read.* Ginn & Co., 1949, Boston, p. 107.
[8] "An Evaluation of Basic-Readers for the School Beginner," *Language Education,* Row Peterson, University Park, 1954.

dull and drab content. Most teachers know that there is something about these books that arouses stories of uncomplimentary nature. This one was told to the author by a mother: A child reading from a primer came upon the following: "Down, down, came the rain, down, down, down." He looked at his mother and snorted, "It would be a funny thing if it went up!"

Basic readers, especially on the lower grade levels, are not often written so that young readers are attracted to them. They most certainly do lack appeal. Still this is no reason for total banishment. Some children *might* find that kind of material useful and will choose it for that reason. The point to be stressed is that a reading program that is basic cannot be restricted to any one or two publications. If this happens, the children whose purposes are not realized must be artificially "motivated" to read such material, and their desire to read is consequently reduced.

3. *Are basal readers true to real life?* An analysis of the content and illustrations of basic readers from a socio-economic class point of view will indicate doubts on this matter. For example, basic readers, with rare exception, portray upper middle class society. The people, their clothing, housing, and their children's playthings are not found in most middle- and lower-class American homes. Even the cleanliness and order of the environment portrayed in these readers (perhaps for purposes of setting good examples) often seem excessive and, in effect, make life as shown in these books seem even further removed from life as most youngsters know it.

4. *Do basal reader systems subordinate the real needs of teacher and student to unrealistic assumptions about the learning-teaching process?* The teaching manuals and workbooks in a basal reader system are designed to compensate for any weaknesses in the readers themselves or in the teaching practices that accompany their use. But even though these de-

tailed teaching aids may at times be quite helpful, they have two serious flaws: They must of necessity assume that all children at a given level have similar reading abilities and weaknesses. They must further assume—else they cannot be termed "basic"—that it is possible to devise teaching-aid material that anyone and everyone can use to equal profit in any given teaching situation. These are, of course, highly unrealistic assumptions.

In addition, supervision has shown that even the modicum of flexibility that manuals suggest is often simply ignored by teachers in basal reading systems. Is it not possible that the climate of day-to-day reliance upon a manual discourages teacher creativity? Is it not possible that manuals discourage teachers from planning their own teaching? In contrast, the teacher in an individualized program finds himself in a climate where he can creatively seize learning opportunities. His judgment and skill and his ability to plan are used because they are needed. Teaching is not a matter of keeping two jumps ahead of the students. Teaching is not mechanical, it is dynamic and alive.

This is not to say that wooden teaching cannot occur in an individualized situation. It can—and does—but not nearly so easily. The nature of the one-to-one relationship is too intensely personal to encourage such practices. The content and method of instruction in an individualized program are not dictated by rigidly required teaching materials. The needs of human beings are not made subservient to what is ostensibly meant to serve them.

5. *Do basic readers sacrifice interesting material in order to control vocabulary?* A trend towards reduction of vocabulary in basic readers has been going on for several years.[9]

---

[9] A. E. Traxler, "Eight More Years of Research in Reading," Educational Records Bureau, New York City, 1955, p. 4.

Drastic cuts in the number of "new" words introduced in successive books in a series have occurred. Concomitantly (and paradoxically) there has been increasing recommendation in reading texts and teaching manuals for teachers to provide enriched collateral reading *in addition* to the required basal reader. New supplementary series have been developed and wider use of trade books has been advocated.

Obviously, basic readers *have* sacrificed interesting content in order to maintain rigidly controlled vocabulary. Otherwise, there would be no need for such strong recommendations for free, collateral reading.

Furthermore, even if students in a basal program do have access to collateral reading, in the course of a school day's tight schedule little time is left for this type of reading. Too often it is the child who is *able* to finish his basal reading and workbook first who gets to do supplementary reading. What about the child who is not such a fast reader and needs all of his time to finish his required work? When does this child have the joy and pleasure of an enriched reading program?

## II  Classroom Organization and Procedure

### A.  Children Choose  What They Read

All teachers know that children will learn more and learn faster when their interest has been aroused. A child can never be forced to be interested in anything. "You can lead a horse to water but you cannot make him drink" fits here, too. But you can stimulate a child's thirst for reading by having a supply of books which attract, beckon, and tantalize. With such a collection teachers need not "motivate" in the usual sense; they act only as a catalyst to bring children and books together. Attractive books, a helpful teacher, and the freedom to browse and select will accentuate the drive to read in children.

High interest is possible for *every* part of the reading program when children choose what they read. To have "work-type" reading and "recreational" reading is to have a dual program. "Work-type" reading is the teacher's program, and "recreational" reading belongs to the child. Yet, if the best elements in both are combined in a free-choice program, no separation or dichotomy need occur.

When teachers choose the books to be read, it is hard for them to fit those books to each child. Thirty-five children in one classroom is 35 times an x number of needs or interests per child, the resultant number running literally into the thousands.[10] Skill or training does not help teachers, parents, or librarians much in trying to be exact in anticipating children's interests in the face of such numbers.

While we have extensive evidence about children's needs and interests and should continually seek more,[11] the problem of getting the "right book to the right child at the right time" is enormously complex. When we fail, books have little appeal and we must "motivate" with all sorts of schemes, devices, tricks and gadgets. When we succeed, children gain the greatest treasure of all—that of wanting to read.

At the outset, children may need help in choosing their reading material wisely. They should be encouraged to choose a book they can read and one that they will like. If more explanation is needed, it should be given. Finding out if it is a book one is able to read means skimming a page or two to see whether there are too many hard words. We can use as a guide "three unknown words to a page," but this is an approximate

[10] In this context see H. S. Bossard, "The Law of Family Interaction." *American Journal of Sociology* (quoted by Willard Olson in *Child Development*. D. C. Heath, Boston, 1949, p. 370).

[11] *See* A. J. Traxler, and A. Townsend, "Eight More Years of Research in Reading." Educational Records Bureau, 21 Audubon Avenue, New York, N. Y., #64, Jan. 1955.

number. If a boy has a book on space travel, for example, there may be six or even more hard words on a page without damaging his interest in that book.

Preventing damage to interest is the key to the whole matter. We *could* let children choose at random. We *could* hand out attractive books indiscriminately, regardless of which child wanted what book. If we followed such a procedure the *sequence of motivation,* which begins with the seeking and selection of a book and ends with its enjoyment and sharing, would be violated. If individualized reading is to be successful, this sequence must be preserved.

In a homogeneous, ability-grouped situation, the drive to read, or the sequence of motivation, starts and ends with the teacher during the reading period. A carry-over of skills into recreational or free-reading is hoped for and planned for, but the sequence is not clear, and reading suffers from a split personality. Some of it is delight and pleasure, but some of it is grim, hard work, all too often in the dullest of all educational material, the basal readers.

In short, choosing books that are liked and that can be read will ultimately help children choose their reading wisely. These are criteria which begin a pattern of reading instruction that will stand squarely on children's purposes and interests. If the drive to read were not so important, these criteria for choosing books would not be so important. But it is, and they are.

## B. Motivation Arises from Child's Interests

When children read to their teacher in an individual conference they are at the peak of a sequence of motivation, for they have selected material that is within their personal interests. On the other hand, when children are arbitrarily placed in slow, medium, or fast reading groups, their personal interests cannot be considered paramount although, of course, a good teacher will do what she can to utilize them.

When we examine teaching procedures in a basal program we usually find the teacher following steps somewhat like these:

1. Developing interest in the story, i.e., "motivating."
2. Anticipating and preparing for difficult words to come.
3. Reading the story silently.
4. Discussing and developing concepts.
5. Working on mechanics.
6. Rereading the story orally.
7. Planning follow-up activities.

In the first step the teacher must try to catch the interest of all members of the group. Every child, whether he wants to or not, must subordinate his own interest to that of the group. If his personal interest does not parallel that of the group, he must be trained to wait passively for a parallel interest to develop in him.

Herein lies a profound philosophical difference between individualized reading and a basal program. In an individualized program, the personal interest of the child is engaged *before* he is taught. In a basal program the interest of the child is subordinate either to the interests of the group or to the material itself.

## C. Instruction on Individual One-to-One Basis

An individual reading conference is, in a sense, an adaptation of the old Mark-Hopkins-on-the-end-of-a-log technique. However, in a classroom, planning and organization are necessary if personal attention is to be given to each child. While one child is with the teacher, the rest of the class must be enough absorbed in an activity to work along with a minimum of interruption of the teacher.

The individual conference period should be the high point

of the entire reading program. All reading roads should lead to it or come from it. If somehow it proves to be unrewarding to the child, the drive to read will be immediately and adversely affected. The better the conference, the better the learning. Instruction is best in these interviews when the teacher has perfected his skills of probing, questioning, and listening. The teacher must develop these skills so as to make the conference valuable, stimulating, and enjoyable, and still fit in the time allotted.

Usually, the following three questions should be explored in each session. (1) How does the child feel about reading in general and his selected piece in particular? (2) What skills need reteaching or developing, and should the child be assigned to a group for instruction or should he be assigned individual independent work? (3) How well does he read orally?

These matters can usually be covered in five minutes with some concentration and practice. The reading period, as a whole, will last from one to two hours depending on the age and grade level of the children, although a longer period is not unusual. Most teachers, once in the swing of things, can hold six to ten individual conferences and three to five instructional or other kind of group sessions in the average reading period.

Students in a reading group on a basal program in the early grades are likely to get but a minute or two of individual attention and even these few minutes are not personal, not private, and are not always available daily to each child. Even at the intermediate grade levels, where reading periods are longer and silent reading receives heavier emphasis than in the lower grades, the amount of undivided, personal attention the teacher gives to each pupil is not great.

Furthermore, identical assignments at each grade level tends to produce boredom in the teacher. To be bored is to lose interest and to lose interest is to de-personalize a situation. When the teaching of reading requires a personal one-to-one conference at frequent intervals, benefit accrues to the teacher as well as to the child.

### D. Grouping Is Short Term, and for a Specific, Immediate Purpose

Individualized reading is based on the psychology of success. It has been said that self-confidence is the *memory* of success. Learning, then, must produce self-confidence to be successful. Goals which are within the grasp of the learner and which tempt him to reach for ever higher and more exciting heights breed confidence. Short term, specific purpose grouping fosters such goals.

Homogeneous grouping has come to have a special meaning in our educational jargon. It refers to separating children within a school or within a class on one or more specific bases—reading achievement, intelligence quotients, age, and so on. But, as a matter of fact, such a group is not homogeneous at all. To set up groups on the basis of something as general as reading achievement scores or reading ability, for example, is really to organize each group on the basis of all the many factors that underlie such ability, which is not homogeneity at all. A truly homogeneous learning group must be organized on a basis of *one, specific, definite criterion that will not change while that group is together*. The common practice of forming 3 or 4 groups of high, medium, or low ability is a most inexact way to organize a classroom if pupil needs are to be met.

Ideally, education should increase differences. If teachers regrouped continually on these differences, the three or four initial groups commonly found would multiply in a short time. An individual program, although probably without self-selection, could be the end result.

But be that as it may, in the usual semi-permanent ability

groupings, the teacher can only direct his teaching in a buck-shot manner and has only a random chance of meeting the explicit requirements of each pupil. The target is too diffuse. In short, each child has too many needs to hope that they can be provided for in such a fashion.

On the other hand, if groups are set up for a carefully desig-nated, single purpose (such as the development of a certain skill, the enjoyment of a particular story, or the remedying of a difficulty) and disbanded when it is accomplished, then the teacher can teach with some hope of meeting pupils' needs. The gifted readers or the slow learners need not be separated into special groups. All of the healthy effects of heterogeneity can be enjoyed without damaging the learning of anyone. Short term, specific purpose grouping is effective because it assures focus on a single target which is within the reach of each mem-ber of the group in the *immediate* future.

### E. Reading Lesson Prepared Independently and Seatwork Has Element of Self-determination

Planning for "seatwork" or independent activities can assure that the children will have enough uninterrupted time to read the book of their choice. When children choose books that they like, they will also be choosing books they can read with a minimum of help. There may be an occasional unknown word or a puzzling idea, but these are likely to present small difficulties. Children absorbed with fine books of their own choosing tend to read independently.

For the seatwork or independent period, the first order of business is for each child to read the book he has selected. This is one of the few mandatory aspects of individualized reading. Reading takes precedence over all other activities until he has "read himself out." When the reading is completed, he decides which *part* of the material he wishes to read aloud to his teacher. When he has made this decision, he spends his seat-work time practicing, alone or with another class member, on the portion of material he wishes to present. (Then, and only then, is he ready for his individual conference.)

From that point on, seatwork or independent activity can take any turn. It *can* be the least valuable of busy work. It also can become a most satisfying intellectual experience.

Teachers can, for example, help children plan activities that lead to other interests. One teacher helped three boys realize that reading a science story about electromagnets could lead to the actual construction of one. Another helped some of her children see that a certain story could be done with hand puppets. They were independently busy for days and it took some doing to pull them back to other classroom subject matter.

When individualizing reading, a teacher develops children's skills in working independently. With teacher approval and guidance they use their own ideas, plan their own activities, and work quietly and purposefully with only a minimum of direction from the teacher.

## F. Remedial Work Integrated with Other Activities

All children, at some time or other, need some kind of instruction, but special remediation is another matter. Unfortunately, remedial reading has come to mean separating the slow readers from their classmates—usually in a different part of the school building. This separation is, of course, a kind of segregation, with attendant emotional stress. The children in such classes are in danger of being publicly stigmatized as stupid or incompetent.

While there are some doubts as to the extent of the effectiveness of remedial reading, the benefits that do accrue are likely to come from the personal attention that children receive in private. Those children who have not received enough personal attention in ability-grouped reading are helped by being taken off by themselves and worked with alone. But if it is recognized that remedial work is beneficial when done individually, although separation from the group has harmful emotional effects, should we not continue working individually but eliminate the stigma of separation?

This is precisely what happens when teachers individualize their reading practice in the classroom. Remedial work is carried on *along with the other activities that are part of the program*. Stigma is sharply reduced or eliminated. Groups exist only long enough to master any one of the many difficulties that arise and are not isolated from the class. Remediation becomes a normal, unmarked part of the reading program.

## G. Planned Sharing Period

When a person has something he likes, he wants to show it off. When children choose their own books, they choose those that they like. They wish others to like them too. One of the phenomena reported by teachers using an individual approach is the development of an end-of-the-reading-period time for "telling about my book." Children get enthusiastic about what they have chosen and want everyone else to know about it. So a more or less planned time for such sharing can hardly be avoided. The delight in certain stories that is exhibited is so communicable that such books become irresistible to other children. This is comparable, in some ways, to the old-fashioned book report, but the activity is voluntary and frequently highly creative. Children like to do it, and since there is no formal writing exercise involved, they do not feel they are being "punished" for reading a book.

Sharing times or "pooling times" are extremely valuable reading activities. There are numerous ways in which books can be shared. Amy Elizabeth Yensen, in the October, 1956,

*Elementary English Magazine,* lists fifty ways without completely exhausting all possibilities. When children love their books, they love to promote them, which, in turn, constitutes another source of inspiration for reading.

## H. Individual's Peak Reading Level Checked and Evaluated

Although the emphasis in an individualized program is on the intrinsic rewards of reading, teachers must have a system of evaluating, checking, or recording the progress of each pupil. And it is true that when every child is reading something different from every other child, we complicate the evaluation task. It is quite possible to keep up with each child, however, if we keep this principle in mind: Only the *best* reading need be checked.

Why should less than the best be evaluated? For that matter why should children be required to read *any* story they are less than sure of? Why should less than the best reading even be considered? When each child has free choice and is reading at his own pace, he presents his story to his teacher *because he is sure he can read it.* He is giving his best or it is within such close reach that the teacher can easily help him attain it. It is up to the teacher, of course, but in an individualized situation this goal is more readily gained than in an ability-grouped situation. Each pupil is reading at his true level of ability and motivated by his true needs and purpose. The teacher evaluates only a *portion* of the child's reading and then proceeds towards improvement. What little time must be spent in waiting to be checked can be used for worthwhile independent reading. No one's time need be wasted.

The teacher has gained a system (see Appendix, pages 238 ff.), the child has achieved success, and records of the child's learning have been made for whatever future purposes they are required. Specific details are noted so that parents, supervisors, administrators or others may know what level of reading achievement each child has attained.

## III  Effects on the Child and on His Reading

### A.  Gifted Child Progresses at His Own Pace

It has been said that the greatest "retardation" among school children today is found among the brilliant pupils. Put another way, it is contended that schools foster mediocrity. Bright children are retarded by the slower pupils. They must wait for them to catch up. To master a skill is a tremendous satisfaction to all human beings. School systems that dull this sense of achievement do a disservice to children.

In individualized reading we find a practice that offers an incentive for the bright child to go as fast as he is able. He does not need to be held back by the slower children in his group. He proceeds at his own rate because the learning situation is such that he can do so freely. Self-selection is the great emancipator of the gifted pupil. He is set free to go as fast and as far as his energy and purpose take him.

### B.  Slow Reader Not Publicly Stigmatized

First-grade texts, second-grade texts, and so on are developed, sometimes on quite arbitrary standards, as a kind of "par" for the particular grade. That is, they are written at the level that authors and publishers, perhaps in collaboration with educationists, feel to be appropriate. Yet some children will not be able to master the reader written for their grade. They must be assigned an easier book or forced to struggle more or less fruitlessly with the one they are supposed to read. These children are usually grouped together. The whole class knows that the group reads easier books or, if they do use the same graded reader, that they read it more slowly. This constant and public reminder of "failure" is, of course, devastating to a child's self-respect. The unhappy psychological effects of such a situation should not be taken lightly. Who is to say that some of the mental illness prevalent in our adult world did not begin with the public humiliation practiced in some of our nation's schoolrooms?

When each child has a different and self-selected book, his difficulties are a matter between himself and his teacher; and no one else need be the wiser. He is working with material geared to his needs, as is everyone else. His failures are private ones and they can be kept that way. Conversely every child, able or not so able, can display his success for all to see. Each child, regardless of ability, can share his story—in his own way, in his own time—with the rest of the class.

## C. Close Personal Interaction with Teacher Serves Child's Psychological Needs

The beneficial effects of working in a close one-to-one situation are obvious. Man needs understanding and he needs a sense of independence, and these needs must be met in the schoolroom, as well as outside, if learning and living are to be effective. There is little disagreement in educational literature on this point. But how do we meet these needs?

The act of teaching is in itself an act of loving and accepting a child. The child who feels he is unimportant to or disliked by his teacher develops blocks toward whatever learning is expected of him. The child who knows he is liked by his teacher finds learning an exciting adventure. It is easier for the teacher to have understanding and love for a child in a one-to-one situation than it is in a ten-to-one situation.

This close relationship with the teacher can also help a child attain the sense of independence that is essential to his proper development. Free choice in reading helps assure successful learning because the goals inherent in this free choice material will be within the chooser's reach. Success will, of course, breed self-confidence. "Self-confidence is the memory of success."

However, the very principle of free choice implies the possibility of wrong choice. The child in an individualized program will make mistakes and will meet with failure. But such experiences will not be traumatic in the warm and friendly atmosphere of close teacher-child relationship. The child's mistakes will not be compounded by neglect or magnified by being publicized to the entire group.

Close personal relationship assures a child the support and "bucking up" that he needs when failure occurs. He can be led to profit by his mistakes. Failure, no less than success, can foster self-confidence when a child learns that *he* can rectify his mistakes, that *he* can rise to the challenge of failure and turn it into success. But, because he is immature, he needs help, ungrudging and personal, if he is to achieve the sense of independence that such triumphs can engender. The close personal relationship of the individualized reading program assures him of just that kind of help.

## D. Reading at Own Interest and Ability Level Fosters Development of Skills

A chance to choose from a rich variety of books and stories will help each child find reading suitable to his own level. But if all the children in a group are forced to read the same book, some of them are certain not to be challenged enough by the material, while some will find it too hard.

A teacher might say, "Yes, but isn't the group level of ability and interest close enough for all practical purposes?" When we have reading practice that enables us to do better than "close enough," why should we settle for less? Individualized reading is structured to fit the child to the book. Ability-grouping has never achieved more than an approximation to this ideal. Reading comes more easily, more rapidly, and becomes more skillful when the book is closely related to the child's purpose and interest.

### E. Acquiring Skills Only as Needed Assures Their Normal Development

All proponents of individual reading are in fundamental agreement that the factor of close interrelationship of teacher and child heightens the sensitivity of the teacher to the child's basic needs. In an individualized approach, children are not taught skills *unless they need them.*

Proponents of basal readers may say, "But each book is carefully *planned* so that a child may go step by step from one level to the next most difficult." This is indeed true. But this carefully planned graduation is more or less useless when the books are used *en masse.* No individual child may pursue *his* step-by-step way *by himself.* He must move along with his peers. A single text cannot fit a dozen children.

In a basal program, all children are taught the skills in regular sequence, according to the teacher's manual, geared to a specific book, in the belief (or hope) that there is a kind of a "natural" order in which reading skills develop. But could it be that these skills are not as sequential as all that? If reading, as most experts tell us, is a highly personal action, perhaps skills develop in quite different sequences in different people. In any event, skills should be taught only when they are needed and *if* they are needed. Otherwise teaching is a waste of time.

A skill should be taught *as each child reveals his need for that skill.* Once a teacher *knows what is needed,* he can proceed to teach it singly, to a group, or to the whole class. The point of the matter is that whatever skill is needed, it is *but one of many*. Its exact place in the development of a certain child cannot be easily anticipated. The child must be allowed to signal its presence. This is possible in one-to-one conference situations. The teacher, then, has his "antennae" waving to pick up these signals which are often subtle and hidden. When they appear, he takes his cue, sets up his lesson, and teaches what is needed. This is indeed teaching. It is on-the-spot, striking while the iron is hot, seizing each teachable moment, and finding satisfaction in watching children grow. When the teacher's purpose and the child's need coincide, learning is effective and teaching is a joy.

### F.  Oral Reading Promoted
###     by Genuine Audience Situation

When children read aloud, their goal is to communicate with their listeners. Expressive use of hands, voice, and face contribute to this communication. It also gives pleasure to the reader. But, when everyone else is silently reading the same words as those being read aloud, what incentive exists to read expressively? In order to develop expressive oral reading, a genuine audience is needed. An audience is a genuine one when it does not know what is coming next and is eager to find out. Thus, the love of being told stories may be transmitted into a desire to learn to read. A genuine audience can be a real incentive to reading and, in addition, serves to promote the art of speaking and of listening.

### G.  Reading Becomes Its Own Reward

To work only for marks, only to beat one's fellows or to please an adult can corrupt a child's desire to learn. Placing a grade on a paper says, in a sense, "This work is not worth doing without a grade. You would probably not have done it if getting this grade had not forced you to do so."

In the field of reading, to read a story from choice is one thing, but to read it because the teacher requires it is quite another. In an individual conference, the teacher accepts and works with the reading matter chosen by the child. If the choice is unwise, the teacher accepts it while he works to improve future choices. But most important of all, the child reads because he wants to read. Teachers can make children do almost anything, but they cannot force enjoyment.

When children do not *want* to read, other measures must be taken. These usually take the form of extrinsic rewards that have nothing to do with reading itself. But extra play time, a grade, a gold star or ribbon have nothing to do with reading itself. And the truth of the matter is that they are only necessary when reading doesn't count for very much by itself.

An exception to this point would be if the reward, after a long work-type reading session, is free-reading itself. This, of course, is not really an extrinsic reward at all. It is, in fact, intrinsic to the basic goal of a good reading program—that is, that reading be considered as pleasurable. Reading that gives personal satisfaction is the kind that begets more reading.

In all the evidence that is accumulating from teachers who have individualized their reading, we find one common thread: *children love to read when they can choose their own books.* It should not be surprising that enthusiasm follows when personal preference is followed. Children themselves feel this keenly. Here are some typical statements made by children who were asked their opinion of an individualized program vis-à-vis a basal one:

"It is is more fun. (i.e., to choose own book)."

"I would rather have a book that I can select myself than one given to me."

"It makes you think."

"If you can read hard books, you can chose a hard one, and if you want an easy book, you can choose it. There's a book for everyone's needs."

"You can read all kinds of exciting books."

"I think this way of reading is better than reading out of readers. When you read out of readers you have to read story after story, and in this kind of reading you can pick up any book you want to. I think that you read more when you read by yourself."

". . . it's better than reading groups because in reading groups you don't learn much. But when you read alone you learn more."

". . . I like it because the reader gets boring and you have to work in a workbook. This way you can read any book that you want and it doesn't get boring."

"I feel happy. In the other school we had to read in groups. And the only way you could read with the teacher was when it's your turn. . . . This way you can read with the teacher by yourself without everyone listening."

"I think this is a good idea. . . . This way you could write to an author, if you have a question about one of the books he wrote. I had that experience and it was good. I wrote to Herman Schneider, several times. After a while as I wrote to him he felt like a brother. The same with Dr. Zim."

Love of reading is the goal of the best teaching of reading. Enthusiasm, eagerness, and high purpose provide evidence of this effect in children. The reading program that is successful is one which sends its pupils out into the world as lovers of books and of all that reading represents.

## PROJECTS AND DISCUSSION TOPICS

### I

A. What is the reasoning behind the system of reading instruction in which an entire class read from the same book on the same page at the same time?

B. What is the reasoning behind a system in which three or four groups read from the same book, although at differing rates per group?

C. What is the reasoning behind a system in which three or four groups use three or four books of varying difficulty?

### Then:

Compare these practices with reference to their efficiency in meeting individual differences.

### II

A. Look up information on the Dalton Plan, the Winnetka Plan, the Pueblo Plan, and the Platoon School.

B. What are the unique characteristics of each?

C. How does each proceed in the individualizing process?

D. How does each compare with that described in this book?

| Chapter | HOW DO WE START? |
|---|---|
| **2.** | |

THIS CHAPTER is designed for teachers who want specific, step-by-step help in setting up individual reading. There are seven major considerations in planning an individualized reading program:

1. Making up your own mind.
2. Consulting with school authorities and parents.
3. Deciding who will participate.
4. Obtaining enough books.
5. Arranging your classroom.
6. Planning the independent work period.
7. Establishing routines.

**The place to start is in your own mind.** Individualizing your reading program is not difficult, even with a large class. But you must decide how much or how little you want to do. You must do only as much as you feel secure in doing.

Erase from your mind the usual pattern of ten or twelve children sitting in a semicircle reading the same page in the same book at the same time. Try to catch the excitement of each child searching through many books to find the one he most wants to read. Think of the variety of books children will bring to you for discussion. Think of how you will teach children to read in many books rather than in the same ones over and over again.

Visualize yourself working with one child. This child has chosen a book that he wants to read from during his conference with you. You and he will have a private reading lesson. You will talk over the story with him; you will hear him read parts of it; if necessary, you will plan special help to improve his reading. When he is finished, another will come for his individual conferences. (You will usually be able to work with six to ten children a day.)

Next, visualize yourself working with a series of small groups. These sessions will be set up to work on short-term projects of all kinds, activities such as writing a class diary, planning a mural, expanding vocabulary, reinforcing skills, or learning a new method of word attack. Once the purpose of the group is accomplished, it is disbanded and another one is formed for another purpose.

Think over these situations and make up your mind whether or not you would like to try this new and different practice. Be sure that it is something you really want to do before you start.

**Second, consult with your school authorities and talk with parents.**

Superintendents, supervisors, and principals are responsible for school curriculum. New ideas should not be tried without their being consulted.

Most administrators are delighted with a show of initiative on the part of teachers and readily lend their support to any new method that has promise. Usually a teacher has but to request permission to experiment and, if his plan is at all reasonable, the go-ahead signal is given.

Parents, too, should have some idea of whatever is to be tried on their children. Teachers would do well to include interested parents in the initial planning for a new idea. Most parents will eagerly accept a plan that promises greater benefits for their children. Administrators and parents alike can be a real source of strength in many ways. There can be tangible effects in increased supplies of books from central offices and loans and donations of books from homes. There can be intangible effects in encouragement and support, which is always helpful to any experimentation.

**The third step is to decide who will participate.** *If you teach first grade* your children are ready to start when they have gained enough skill in word recognition and word analysis to read independently in beginning books. If you can get children ready to read in groups, you can get them ready to read on an individual plan. The reading readiness activities which prepare children for preprimers and primers of a basal series can serve in a nonbasal program also.

However, if you have children who have not yet reached the point where the beginning books can be used, you must provide other kinds of experiences for them. Do not expect such children to read independently. They are not yet ready for that. But neither do they need to hold up your plans to adopt a different kind of reading practice. Their needs can be met in other ways, such as working with charts, doing practice exercises of many kinds, and other reading readiness activities.[1]

Since the acquisition of a sight vocabulary must precede independent reading, you should display your supply of books in a prominent place. Refer to or read from certain ones and urge children to "go and look" when they can. You will notice that some children show intense interest in these books. Encourage them to take them freely to look at or to try to read. Praise

[1] See D. Lamoreaux, and D. M. Lee, *Learning to Read Through Experience*. New York, Appleton-Century-Crofts, 1943; and Marion Monroe, *Growing Into Reading*. Chicago, Scott Foresman, 1951, for a comprehensive discussion of this subject. Also see pp. 61-88 of present volume.

them when they show you words that they recognize on their own. Combine such activities with the "regular" classwork and soon many children will be at a level where they can read beginning books independently. Then you are ready to proceed individually.

Start with those children who show their readiness this way. The rest can follow later. If you are in doubt about a child's reading level, the following information will be helpful.

Laura Zirbes [2] found that children who read slower than sixty words a minute orally and make more than two serious errors in that time do not find independent reading pleasant, interesting, or profitable. Betts [3] indicates that the "levels of independence" are achieved when the pupil meets one "new" word per two hundred at the primary level and one "new" word for one hundred at the intermediate level.

Tests are another tool that can be used to judge reading readiness, although this writer feels that if testing readiness for a basal series and readiness for self-selected books could be separated, the results would be quite different.

Mental age is another criterion by which some teachers decide when children are ready to read. But if your school uses mental age as a criterion, especially when it is based on a test involving verbal ability, you should be aware of the reservations of some educators concerning its use. Gates, for example, doubts the validity of using mental age for this purpose. He says that "statements concerning the necessary mental age at which a pupil can be intrusted to read are meaningless. The age of learning to read under one program or with the

[2] *Practice Exercises and Checks on Silent Reading in the Primary Grades. Report of Experimentation.* New York, Lincoln School of Teachers College, Columbia University, 1925.

[3] National Society for Study of Education. *Reading in the Elementary School.* 48th Yearbook, Pt. II, Chapter XIII, Emmett R. Betts, "Adjusting Instruction to Individual Needs," p. 274.

method employed by one teacher may be entirely different from that required under other circumstances." [4]

Perhaps the best check of all in ascertaining which children are ready to read will come from your own observation and judgment. You are the one closest to the children and are consequently in a position to recognize when a child is signaling his readiness to read. Children have ways of letting you know when they are ready for any new learning. Some continually ask questions about books. Some follow you around asking about words they find. Some will make up games pretending to be learning to read. These are a few of the indications which tell you it is safe to proceed. These are the ways you will know which children should participate in any reading program.

*If you teach an intermediate grade* achievement level can be checked by means of tests or by having a child read in a succession of books in a basic reader series. Information thus gained will help you when securing books and will also be a guide during your early individual conferences.

The change-over from set reading groups to independent, self-selected reading can be done by one group at a time or by the whole class at once. Many teachers have shifted their class as a unit without any difficulty at all. But you may find it easier to slip gradually, group by group, from a familiar pattern into this new one.

Teachers who have begun with only one group have given various reasons for doing so. Some chose their best readers on the theory that their highly developed reading skills would weather even an unsatisfactory experiment. Others chose their slowest readers, reasoning that these children had nothing to

[4] A. I. Gates, "The Necessary Mental Age for Beginning Reading." *Elementary School Journal* 37:497-508, 1937. Also quoted p. 988, *Encyclopedia of Educational Research.*

lose but their inability to read. And some teachers chose the members of their beginning group for quite arbitrary reasons of their own.

Shifting from ability grouping to free-choice reading seems a tremendous task to some teachers. If it strikes you that way, it will probably be better for you to proceed with few children at a time until you gain confidence. After all, you will be moving in the direction of individualization if you merely let children read on different pages of their basal readers—and that is no trick at all.

**The fourth consideration is to increase your supply of books.** You must have a *minimum* of three different titles per child, and the program works better when there are even more books available.

First-grade teachers will need books for children with abilities ranging from the picture books of the earliest prereading levels to books of at least third-grade material. As the range will increase as the year goes by, the difficulty levels of materials can be increased as needed.

Teachers in the intermediate grades will want to select books that are somewhat below the achievement level of the slowest readers and a grade or two above the highest achievement level. Such a wide range is necessary to guarantee that all will have a choice under all conditions. Do not be surprised if your book supply comes to have a difficulty range of six or seven grades. This is not at all unusual and reflects the span of ability in average classroom groups, especially above the third grade— which is one reason why a self-selection program is so satisfying to widely heterogeneous groups.

To obtain one hundred and twenty or more books at one time takes a bit of doing. Here are some suggestions as to how you might proceed.

1. Order trade books [5] on your regular book order.
2. Order one or two copies of supplementary readers that you do not already have.
3. Order one or two copies of basal readers you do not already have.
4. Sound out your P.T.A. or teachers' organization about having a Book Fair.[6]
5. Trade some of your books with other teachers for those you do not have.
6. Visit all libraries within a reasonable distance and inquire how to obtain boxes of books on loan and about their policy of selling "throw-outs."
7. Request bookmobile visits and be persistent until they are made.
8. Write or visit state and county libraries or other tax-supported book depots and request the loan of boxes of books. Refer unreasonable refusals to your local legislative representative.
9. Take your class to the library and be sure each pupil has his own personal library card.
10. Encourage every child to use his own library card.
11. Encourage children to bring books from home.
12. Hunt through second-hand book stores or stores of service organizations, and attend sales at church bazaars and the like.
13. Thoroughly explore your school's storeroom or that of the central office.
14. Ask for book samples which principals, supervisors or administrators frequently receive.

[5] This is a publisher's term that means books that are not texts.

[6] Help in planning book fairs is available from these sources: Scholastic Teacher, 33 W. 42nd St., New York 36, N. Y., "Manual on Book Bazaars" (50¢). Children's Book Council, 50 W. 53rd St., New York 19, N. Y., "How to Run a Book Fair" ($1.50). Library Journal, 62 W. 45th St., New York 36, N. Y., "Books to Build On" ($2).

15.  Institute a book hunt in your own and other people's
attics.

In short, hunt everywhere you can think of and reject no
book that might be suitable for your children. There will be
trade books and basal readers, fairy tales, and science fiction,
books of fact, books of adventure, biographies and tall tales.
All are to be welcomed.

The main point is to get plenty of books. Subject matter
should be exceedingly varied. Try to anticipate all of the possible reading interests of your class. You can get rid of the
books that children don't "take to" later on. Involving the
children in this treasure hunt also serves to increase their
interest in the reading activity that is to come. There is no need
to make this activity a secret! When you have one hundred to
one hundred and fifty books for the free choice of your class,
your supply is adequate and you are ready for the next step
in preparing to individualize your teaching of reading.

**Fifth, look at your classroom arrangement.** Find a place
for the books where a number of children can come to make
their choice without crowding each other. A large table, or
long, wide shelves will serve the purpose. If the children's seats
are movable, arrange them in such a way that the books are
easily available.

Appropriate a quiet corner for yourself with a chair *beside*
your own. Children respond better when they are alongside,
not opposite their teacher. Perhaps you will want to sit at a
table, but, in any case, there should be some degree of privacy.
It is important to be able to work with a single child without
the others being aware of the content of your conversation.
Finally, check to see if children can move to and from the book
supply and to and from your corner with reasonable ease. If this
is possible, your room is arranged suitably for an individualized
program.

**Sixth, plan for independent activities.** Independent activities are particularly important if you are to work with a minimum of interruption during the reading period. Many teachers begin their school day with a planning session, which helps children use their self-selected book for further independent work. As this material is always to be the first activity of all children during the period, it provides rich opportunities for a sustained experience. A boy may read a book on adventure, and then follow it up with a puppet show as a way of sharing his reading with the class. Two friends may find a poem they would like to memorize and recite. A science experiment may result from reading a book on science.

You can, if you wish, carry on exactly the same kind of seatwork as you are accustomed to under any other kind of a reading program—with one exception: the *first* independent activity of each child should be to read his self-chosen material silently. Perhaps you would rather stay with the kind of seatwork that is familiar to you until you notice the children are gaining ability to work independently, at which time you can try tying the self-selected book in with other activities.

Even though it is true that seatwork need be little different under a basal and individual program, differences do arise because part of the period is spent on silent reading of a self-selected book. The intense interest in free-choice materials produces greater concentration on the part of pupils and tends to free teachers from lock-step work-book or blackboard practice exercises. You will find your "seatwork" period more purposeful and productive.

Here are some suggestions for wise and creative use of pupil time when independent activities are indicated:

- An autobiography replete with snapshots
- A class diary (done by an individual, by friends, a small group, or the whole class)

- A class newspaper
- A cumulative story book
- Letters to sick absentees, to grandparents, brothers in the service, or to a local place of business which has something interesting·to see
- Some creative writing
- Social or friendship grouping of three or more children around a worthwhile self-developed interest
- A social studies report
- Fact finding for a news report
- Preparation for a news discussion
- Directions for construction of an electromagnet, water clock, or some other device
- A group dramatization
- Choral speaking (friends, small group, or whole class)
- Keeping all kinds of records—library books, milk money, growth of classroom plants, a scientific experiment
- A puppet show involving making of puppets as well as writing scripts or outlining dialogue
- Labeling pictures, scrapbook, album, etc.
- Developing hobbies or any worthwhile special interest

**Seventh and final step, establishing routines.** Beyond arranging for the physical environment of your classroom and planning independent activities with your pupils, you must establish routines so that the whole reading period runs smoothly. Some routines are simple and require little more than initial directions; for example, how and when to get a new book and return the old one. Other routines are more complex and need more detailed directives and closer supervision on your part. Children's records of their own reading, for instance, will need periodic checking to insure that all is well.

Classroom procedures are always smoothed by a systematic

approach. This is especially true in working to help children with words they do not know. There will not be as many such words as you might anticipate, because the children themselves will have chosen books with only a few unknown words a page. The high interest factor also helps children make better use of context and picture clues than when they read less interesting material. However, there will be children who come upon words they do not know, and a system is needed to help them find their meanings. Some primary teachers put picture dictionaries in convenient places and see that experience charts and stories are hung on the walls where children may go through them for remembered phrases that will help. Higher grade teachers also use various dictionaries, appropriate kinds of familiar material, and other helpful devices.

Children themselves can be used on a volunteer basis as "word helpers," although they should not be used too frequently. Teachers can, of course, instruct the children to come to them quietly and point out the difficult word. There are many other ways that may occur to you to deal with this situation. In passing, it should be mentioned that some teachers make quick records of words that require explanation and include them in later vocabulary study. Children can also be coached to do the same if it does not retard their motivation to read.

It is surprising how resourceful children become in helping themselves work out unknown words when they are personally committed to what they are reading. One first-grade teacher recorded the following conversation about some reading a child had done at home.

"How did you figure out the words you did not know?"

"I thought and thought of words that began with 't' and 'd' (which were the beginning letters of the unknown words) until I thought of a word that fit."

Another first grade teacher reported that one child, although he had hitherto failed every formal and informal reading readiness measure, appeared before her with a preprimer and read it through correctly.

"How did you know all of the words? You didn't ask for help."

"Oh, I saw all those kids reading to you by themselves and I wanted to read to you, too. So I got this book and figured out the words from the pictures and asked Joe for a couple. It wasn't very hard."

## Check List for Teachers Preparing to Individualize Reading

1. Is my own mind made up?
2. Do I know the reading level of my pupils?
3. Have I decided who will participate?
4. Do I have enough books?
    a. Are there three to five per child?
    b. Are there no more than three or four of the same title?
    c. Is there a wide enough range of difficulty for all needs at all times?
    d. Are there enough subjects to interest everyone?
5. Is my room ready?
    a. Are books easily available?
    b. Do I have a good place for individual conferences?
    c. Can pupils sit beside me?
    d. Is there a place for small groups to meet?
    e. Can traffic move reasonably freely?
6. Have I planned enough for readers and nonreaders to do while I work with individuals and groups?
7. Have I established adequate routines?
    a. Do I have a plan for getting and returning books?
    b. Do I have a plan for keeping records?

    c.  Have I planned a way to help with unknown words?

    d.  Have I planned other routines for my room?

8.  Have I consulted with school authorities and parents?

## Introducing the New Program

There are two ways in which you can change a basal ability-grouped program into one which is individualized. One, you can change over part of your class or one group of your class at a time. Two, you can change the entire class at one time.[7]

### One-Group-at-a-Time Change-over

You will take your first steps towards individualizing reading during the regular reading period of the group that you have decided will participate. The rest of the class will continue without change. Independent seatwork will be carried on as usual.

At first, increase the amount of silent reading in the change-over group and decrease the amount of oral reading. Encourage, or at least do not prevent, children reading on ahead of the rest of the group. Give praise and encouragement when you notice children proceeding through their book rapidly and with comprehension.

Work on skills at the end of the period and then deal only with what proved to be most difficult in what was read. Take notes on each child. You may, at first, have everyone work on skills, but try not to have any child wait while you teach a skill that he already knows. Gear each day's skill session more and more to the needs of each pupil until the time comes when each is on the individual plan and the group is disbanded.

---

[7] There are many patterns that can be developed from these two ways. In addition to those described below, several others are described in Part II. The reader is also referred to Celia Stendler's "The Ritual of Primary Reading" in *Elementary English,* March, 1948.

As the days pass, encourage each child to come to you when he is ready. As the rest read on silently, have him read a part of the story he has selected—the "best" part, the "funniest" part, etc. Discuss the story with the child, enjoy it with him, ask him to tell you what happens next or what has preceded. In this way you set up a personalized teaching situation and children will come to recognize your genuine interest in what they are doing.

When a child finishes the basal text (or when he shows boredom with it), invite him to take another book from those that have been accumulated. Soon every child will have finished the basal book, or will at least be reading a different page of it than is any one of his fellow students. Thus all will be reading a different piece of material, and you will be in a position to teach each one individually without resorting to group teaching at all unless you so desire.

## Whole Class-at-a-Time Change-over

When you change an entire class from an ability-grouped procedure to an individual pattern, begin by an explanation of what is to happen.

You might say something like this: "Girls and boys, today we are going to do our reading differently. Over here, as you can see, we have many new, exciting, and interesting books. For your reading today you are to choose one of these books that you like and take it back to your seat to read. Do not choose a book that is too hard for you. When you see one that looks interesting, turn to any page in it and see if you know most of the words. If there are more than three on that page that you don't know, you'd probably be wise to choose another book. Now let's choose our books."

Have as many children as can be accommodated at a time come and get their books. When everyone has his book and is back at his seat, you can discuss the problems in book selection that have arisen. Maybe some have chosen books that are too difficult. Others may have chosen those that are too easy. Still others may have taken just the first one they picked up.

When you are satisfied that all understand what "self-selection" implies, continue with your explanation: "Read the book you have chosen as long as you like. Ask me [or one of the word helpers] about any words you need to know. I will be sitting over here with a chair beside me. When you have read your book, go back over it, and pick out one part that you would like to read aloud to me. Be sure you know all about it and can tell me what happens in it. Read it several times so I will hear your best reading. Then come to me and we will read, just you and I together. If someone is here ahead of you, you can just sit off to the side and practice your story while you are waiting."

Then you might walk one or two children through the whole procedure so that all can see how it goes. When you are satisfied that everyone understands, you have made your start. Place yourself in a spot where you have some degree of privacy, but can still lean back to whisper words to children who need them.

## The Individual Conference

If all is running smoothly with each child settled with a book that he likes and can read (and your independent work has been planned), you are ready to retire to your chosen spot with notebook in hand and wait for volunteers. Some teachers put up a list of the names of the children who have already indicated their readiness for their individual conference. Other teachers take volunteers first and organize an "on deck" arrangement so that each will have a fair chance to read. One of the pleasures of individualizing reading is to see the eagerness with which children beg for their turn with their teacher. Children

Oral reading during an individual conference: a happy highlight of the individualized reading program.

*Leal School, Urbana, Illinois*

Self-selection in practice. Note display of book jackets supplied free by publishers.

(This and all following illustrations are used through the courtesy of Principal Mortimer J. Abramowitz and the faculty of Public School 167, Brooklyn, New York.)

Reading self-selected books as first job of independent work period.

Independent activities are varied. This picture shows a small group at work on a play, while others are reading, writing, painting or helping each other.

Determining child's approximate reading level by using a basal series as an informal test. The teacher also notes strengths and weaknesses upon which to base later teaching and short-term grouping activities.

Individual conference to aid in perfecting the mechanics of reading. This teacher is providing the help the child needs on a particular phase of phonics. (Note the teacher's 5 x 8 record cards on her desk.)

Short-term group. The teacher shown is working with a small group having a common difficulty with suffixes. She is using a particular page in a work book, designed to help children overcome this problem.

Whole class skill session. Using a trade book to develop in second graders the idea of sequence in a story.

Record keeping by children: a display in a fifth grade class. Children keep records of books read. They make short notations on 3 x 5 cards, which are kept in the envelopes on the wall. (Note the display of letters from authors.)

Sharing time. These boys have made paper puppets and are acting out a story with them.

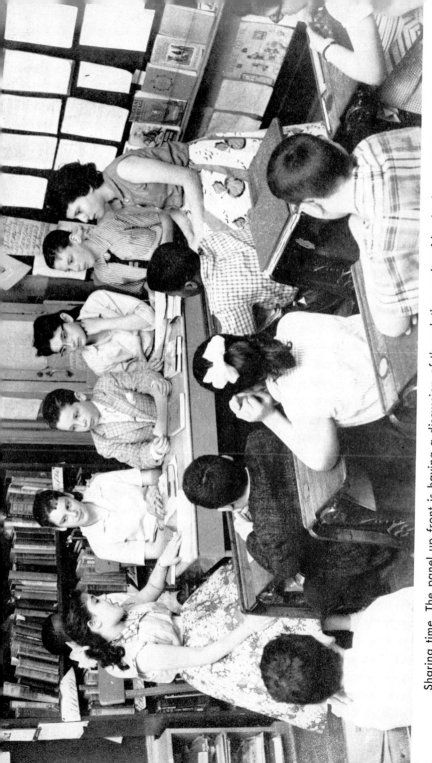

Sharing time. The panel up front is having a discussion of the relative merits of books the pupils have read.

Sharing time. This fourth grader is telling about her book. (Note the cage of mice as a "prop".)

will object strongly if they consider they have been unfairly passed over as far as the individual conferences are concerned.

It is interesting that most teachers agree that conferences should be held on a voluntary basis. Having children come by alphabetical order, or by rows or tables, seems to have an immediate inhibiting effect on their interest in their reading. Evidently a child's decision as to when he is ready to come for individual conference is important to his motivation to read.

Should a child come to his conference unprepared, you must gently but firmly send him back. Be sure he knows exactly what is wrong: perhaps he was in too much of a hurry to choose a book, perhaps the book was too hard, etc.

Any alert teacher will follow up a child who does not seem eager to come for his conference. If there is a consistent lack of eagerness, it could be a signal that something is wrong with the motivational sequence. Maybe there are not enough books or not enough *interesting* books. It could be that the individual conference does not seem important to the child. (Perhaps you, yourself, have not emphasized it enough!)

Usually, however, there will be little sign of reticence. As one teacher put it: "They are yanking at my skirts *all* the time. 'Can I read to you now?' 'Can I read to you now, *please?*' And I just have to figure out ways to do it."

## The Use of Questions in the Individual Conference

At last the time arrives when the first child appears with his prepared material. He sits down and you begin his instruction in reading.

There are three aspects of reading that you need to investigate during each conference. Any and all of these can lead to productive group work later on:

1. The pupil's understanding of and reaction to his chosen piece of material.

2. The pupil's ability to deal with the mechanics of reading.
3. The pupil's ability to read orally (the climactic point in the session).

These aspects are explored best by (1) your careful use of open-ended questions and (2) your being an interested and appreciative listener. Open-ended questions are those which are difficult to answer with "yes" or "no." They require a bit of skill on the part of the teacher. For example, the question, "Did you like this story?" may bring either "Yes" or "No" as an answer. But to ask, "What kind of a story is this?" should bring a response that can not be so easily encompassed in one word. This kind of question produces better teaching results because the answer gives you more information about the pupil's reading and allows the child to "talk out"—and thereby "think out" —his reactions.

Open-ended questions tend to bring forth information with little or no prodding or probing by the teacher. Compare these two questions and their possible answers:

1. "Show me the page where so-and-so did thus-and-so."
2. "Why do you think so-and-so is a funny character in this story?"

In the first question, the pupil would show the page requested and the question would be answered. Not so in the second question, where the pupil might indicate several instances to document his answer to the question. The very nature of the second question requires much more information and much more thought than is the case with the first.

But open-ended questions should not attempt to lead a pupil to an answer desired by the teacher. A child should not be made to feel he must guess what is in his teacher's mind in order to please her. He should be allowed to form his own judgments without necessarily reflecting those of others.

To illustrate this point, let us compare these two questions:
1. "The Little Red Hen worked hard, didn't she?"
2. "How do you feel about Little Red Hen?"

In the first question the pupil has little choice but to agree that Little Red Hen did work hard. This is an example of a leading question. On the contrary, the second question allows a pupil to have an opinion of his own and to express it. He is not led into an answer.

The following questions are good examples of the kind that will help you investigate the three aspects of reading.

1. *The pupil's understanding of and reaction to his chosen piece of material.* "Why did you choose this book?"—"Which character did you like best?" "Why?"—"How did you know what kind of a character so-and-so is? Show me where it says so."—"Did you like to read this story? Why?"—"What kind of a book is this? Fact or science story, funny story, fairy tale, or what?"—"Tell me the story."—"What is the best part of the story?"—"What comes next after so-and-so does so-and-so?"

For the intermediate grades, more detailed content-area questions can be asked. For example: "What is different about sailboats on the Nile River than here in America?" The type of material, of course, dictates the kind of questioning to pursue.

2. *The pupil's ability to deal with the mechanics of reading.* "Was this book hard for you, easy for you, or just right? How can you tell?" (If the answer indicates that it was hard or easy, you will probe further for reasons.) "How do you know that you are reading better than you did?" "What words did you get stuck on?" (Proceed to help in their analysis.) "Were there any words that you didn't know at first but later figured out? How did you do it?"

Further questions could explore the child's ability to note details, to make inferences, to predict events, to see relationships, and the like. Again we note that the type of material dictates the type of questioning. A vivid, dramatic story generally requires little attention to the mechanics of the reading process. However, children reading a description of an historical event do need training in certain mechanics in order to understand such material fully.

3. *The pupil's ability to read orally.* Little questioning is needed to evaluate the children's ability to read aloud. You have already probed his ability to read silently, so now you can sit back and prepare to be an interested and appreciative audience. You could proceed as follows: "What have you chosen to read to me today?" "Why did you choose this part to read aloud?"

If a child asks, "What shall I read?" you might answer in this vein: "The best reading you can do. Choose something that seemed funny to you, or exciting. But be sure it is something you can read very well."

As the child reads, you listen and watch. Does he read smoothly? Does he sound as if the story has meaning to him? Does he laugh at its funny parts? Does his voice change its inflection? Do you find yourself following the story with interest? If so, your pupil reads well. The purpose of reading aloud is to communicate to an audience. During the individual conference you are that audience. Later on, perhaps, the class will be his audience. Oral reading is the culmination of all the child's preparation. It is the reward for all of his work. It is his time to shine, first in front of his teacher, and then for an interested group of his peers.

As the individual conference draws to a close you will decide what further work the child needs. Perhaps he is having trouble with short vowel sounds. If so, he will need to join with several others in similar difficulties during the portion of the reading period set aside for groups and work with them to improve his word attack skill. Or perhaps the child is one of several who would profit by dramatizing a particular story. Or you may feel that this child would benefit particularly from the experience of helping to develop a class diary in order to enrich his vocabulary.

As each child reveals different needs, you must be alert to make the proper assignment to improve his reading skills. Each individual conference should end on this note of further work and higher goals.

Finally, to make sure you have accomplished what you set out to do, check yourself with these questions.

1. Has he read well silently? Did he understand what he read?
2. Have I improved the mechanics of his reading?
3. Did he read well orally?
4. Did I plan for later activities?
5. Would he benefit by working out a special assignment? Alone? With a group?

As you end each conference, make a record of the pertinent data, do whatever evaluating you wish, and let the next child take his place.

## Ways of Evaluating and Recording

The reading progress of your students may be evaluated in various ways. You may wish to use standardized achievement tests. You may rely on the evidence of increasing competence with difficult material or increased reading activity in general. Some teachers have pupils read portions of successive books in a basal series and note whether or not reading ability has improved.

### Teacher's Records

You will need a ledger, a loose-leaf notebook, or a file of 5″ x 8″ cards. Each child will have a page or card of his own.

Most teachers list name, age, reading achievement, test scores, and other information that may be needed. Most teachers keep these notes confidential, but this is a matter of personal preference.

As each child comes to you, you will keep a record of his individual conference with the date. You may write as the conference proceeds, or you can wait until its end if you wish. You should record what you consider important to remember: individual or group assignments, books or pages read, difficulties revealed ("Trouble with reading quotations" "Skips around too much") or an unusually emphatic reaction ("I just *love* horse stories!"). A note to yourself ("Needs help with vowel sounds" or "Must help him find more challenging material") may help you plan for the next day.

You should also keep records, in a separate part of your notebook or file box, of independent activities and sharing-time activities—dramatizations, choral speaking, panels, exhibits, etc. (See Appendix.)

### Children's Records

Children themselves can keep track of each book or part of a book read. They can keep a diary, or a record of their reading in a file or notebook, listing simple and previously agreed upon items: title and author of book, date taken and returned, a brief comment. More detailed records are sometimes kept by children when there is some particular need or interest, but children should never be coerced into doing so—they should never be made to feel that they are being punished for finishing a book.

Formal required "book reports" are almost guaranteed to weaken a child's interest in reading. However, voluntary oral or written comments or reports by the children (and perhaps typed up by an adult) which attempt to "sell" the book can greatly strengthen interest.

You should ask to see the children's records periodically. You may want to see each child's during the individual period, or you may wish to review and record them all at one time. (See Appendix.)

## Partial Individualization

If you feel you would rather proceed in even slower stages than those suggested above you can make some moves in the direction of individualization without committing yourself completely to the new program at the outset.

Here are some suggestions:

1. *Self-selection.* Since free choice of material is the goal, you can make a first step by letting the members of any one of your groups choose their own stories from the group's reader for one day and see what happens. Or, you might have everybody read as usual from a basal text in the morning and from self-selected books in the afternoon, with some time allowed for oral reading to you or to the whole class. But remember that to the extent that you are choosing the selection, you are not allowing the self-selection process to motivate reading.

2. *Individual Conferences.* You can hear individual children read at odd moments that your schedule allows. *Any* time your whole class is busy and does not need you for several minutes could be used to hear individual pupils read. This could be during a recreational reading period, during a workbook assignment period, or during a catching-up time in a subject other than reading.

3. *Group sessions based on other than ability.* If your class is divided into three or four groups based upon reading ability, you can vary that arrangement, even if only for one day. You might ask for volunteers to write a class diary. Or, children

in the group who may have identical difficulties—such as inability to recognize a central idea or to read aloud with expression—may be taken from their reading group for corrective practice.

## PROJECTS AND DISCUSSION TOPICS

### I

A. Canvass your community for resources that can be used by teachers in hunting for books.
B. Write to resources outside of your community (public and private, county, state and national) which can assist teachers in expanding their book supplies.

Then:

Pool all of your information, discuss its meaning for education in your community, and make some decision as to its dissemination.

### II

Read a primer and its accompanying manual and workbook of several basic series.

Then:

Develop lessons similar to those found in a workbook for a well-known trade book. Try them out on children. Discuss the results.

# Part II

## INDIVIDUALIZED READING
## IN ACTION

*The following articles have been chosen for their importance in the development of the concept of individualized reading. In addition they are replete with descriptions of classroom practice. A teacher wishing to change from a basal reading program to one using the self-selection process will find here many and various practical applications of the ideas discussed in Part I.*

*The introductory statement for each article may be used as a guide to indicate grade level or the particular aspect of individualized reading under discussion—ways of selecting books, keeping records, and so on. In this way a classroom teacher may select the materials most helpful to him and most suitable to the stage of development of his particular program.*

# TEACHING READING
# IN THE ELEMENTARY SCHOOL

*Staff of Maury School,*
*Richmond, Virginia*

*This material, published in 1941, is an excellent presentation of a reading program that is not dependent upon ability groups or basic readers. It will be particularly useful to teachers who wish to know more about developing reading material from children's experiences. The many examples of children's communications show how school life can be deeply involved in teaching and learning. The complete pamphlet, of which the article reproduced here is a portion, was prepared under the editorship of Marion Y. Ostrander.*

## Reading Skills Develop Best in a Well-planned Scheme of Day-by-Day Living

THE READING PROGRAM of a school must, first of all, be considered in relation to the community as a whole. Taking this into account, the school staff seeks to know the parents of the children as friends and to work with them, in season and out, to contribute something to the enrichment of life for the people of the community. Much emphasis has been placed upon creating beauty in the environment of the children. Moreover the primary consideration in facing any school problem is to increase the security and happiness of the children, and this can be done only in the framework of their daily life with their families as well as with their school associates.

Reprinted with permission of the American Education Fellowship.

The reading program must, secondly, be considered in relation to the whole school program. The school is thought of as a community where persons concerned (parents, teachers, children) live and work together attempting to solve some of the problems that face them. Effort is made to manage the affairs of the school community so that each person, the youngest child or the oldest parent, may have a share in planning and doing things that are important to the group. The quality in this kind of effort has been constantly increasing with the growth in creative leadership among staff members. This growth in leadership has resulted from continuous experience in guiding persons to carry on their own purposeful endeavors. It has been guided by a long range view of society and its goals rather than by artificial, arbitrarily imposed standards.

## Reading Grows From the Life of the School

Having in mind such a scheme of day-by-day living, cooperatively planned and carried out, Maury School provides many experiences rich in educational value for children, teachers and parents. Glaring shortages in the community are viewed as resources to stimulate effort. For example, because of unfortunate residential conditions, health is a vital problem to be dealt with and nutrition has an important bearing upon wholesome development. Therefore, the whole issue of eating in school must be thoughtfully faced. With only eight wash basins available for the 450 children in the school it took careful planning to find opportunity for regular hand washing before lunch each day. One group of third grade children took the responsibility of compiling the recommendations coming from the whole group. The following is a sample of the sheets finally sent to each room:

YOUR ROOM WILL USE BASIN NUMBER ONE BE-
TWEEN 12:00 AND 12:10. PLEASE USE ONLY ONE

TOWEL AND PLACE IT IN THE TRASH CAN WHEN
YOU FINISH.
PLEASE LEAVE THE SOAP IN THE STAND WHERE
YOU FIND IT.

Though the big children did the writing and reading, the little children were no less aware of the problem confronting them. Therefore, they were experiencing communication by means of the printed word.

Several children assume responsibility for the music during the lunch hour. They select a victrola record before the lunch hour each day and play it at the proper time. In order that the children may enjoy it more, the committee often write a notice about the selection to be played with some comment concerning it. This is functional reading, writing and spelling.

Each Friday morning, menus for the following week are prepared for parents and children. Hunter, one of the boys in charge of the music, sent the following letter on the menu one week:

DEAR MOTHERS
   I AM TAKING CARE OF THE MUSIC IN THE CAFE-
TERIA NOW. MY MOTHER CAME AND ATE LUNCH
WITH ME ONE DAY LAST WEEK. SHE ENJOYED IT
VERY MUCH. THE TEACHERS AND THE CHILDREN
WOULD ENJOY HAVING YOU EAT WITH THEM SOME-
TIME.
                    YOUR FRIEND
                    HUNTER

This letter touched close to home to every child in school. Although not all could actually read it, it functioned as a means of communication and was therefore good reading material.

A group of 5½-year-olds entered school for the first time. They set out to learn about the people who helped run this school. They visited the cook and talked with her about her work. They talked with the maids, who explained what their work was and how the children might help. They went to the furnace room with the janitor who helped them to understand his job. They interviewed the principal in the office and asked her what she did. They summarized their findings in this chart which the teacher wrote:

FLORENCE IS THE COOK.
SHE COOKS GOOD FOOD FOR THE CHILDREN.
MR. FERGUSON IS THE JANITOR.
HE MAKES FIRES IN THE BIG FURNACES.
GLADYS IS THE MAID.
SHE HELPS US CLEAN OUR ROOM.
MISS BAILEY IS THE PRINCIPAL.
SHE ANSWERS THE TELEPHONE.

Reading, writing and spelling are here interwoven in functional usage. The children supplied the content for the chart. As the teacher read it aloud, running her hand from left to right under the words, the children experienced the beginning of eye movements in reading. Gradually they assumed more and more of the responsibility of recording their experiences.

Day by day alert individuals point out things of interest to the whole school. For example children and teachers decided that the best means of bringing news to all was to ask each class to take turns in flashing daily headlines before the whole school. One day this chart appeared in a central place:

POP IS CLEANING UP THE PLAYGROUND.
IT WILL OPEN TUESDAY.
HE GAVE MARY ALICE THESE FLOWERS.

The flowers were placed in a bowl by the chart. Pop was a friend of all the children and they were delighted to know that the neighborhood playground was opening. During the day as children passed through the hall, it was interesting to see groups gathering at the chart, the older children reading to the younger ones.

Another day this announcement appeared:

COME ON EVERYBODY!
LET'S ALL GO DOWN TO MILLER AND RHOADS THIS
AFTERNOON TO THE BOOK FAIR.
LOIS LENSKI WILL BE THERE.

That very morning Lois Lenski had gone from room to room talking with the children. An author now was real and of course everybody wanted to go to Miller and Rhoads.

One day the children read this on the school news stand:

IT IS BIG AND WHITE.
IT WILL KEEP OUR FOOD COOL.
HAVE YOU SEEN THE NEW REFRIGERATOR IN THE
CAFETERIA?

These, with others like them, illustrate the use of common experiences in building group consciousness. *The more interesting the things children do, the better they read.*

Day after day teachers help children to see the importance of nice living in the simple everyday things of life. Dignity surrounds dining in the cafeteria. The children help to keep the room beautiful by painting murals for the walls. Fresh flowers are placed on the tables each day. Colorful curtains hang at the windows. It is a bright, cheerful place. Boys and girls take pride in leaving it clean for the groups that come after them. Good reading materials come out of many of their discussions regarding the lunch hour. For illustration, a chart in one room read:

"EXCUSE ME, JOHN.
I'M SORRY I KNOCKED OVER YOUR MILK.
I WILL GET YOU ANOTHER BOTTLE."

This was a conversation between two children at the table overheard by the teacher. As the class read it, John recognized his own name. It was probably the only word he did recognize but the important fact is: *John was reading*. Whether the child is five years old or eight, the teacher makes sure whenever he meets a reading situation that he gets the feeling of the whole reading experience. She may help him over difficulties by supplying words he does not know. She may help make meanings clear. She may help keep his interest alive. She never lets word-calling kill his effort. This is to say that she never permits an emphasis on one phase of reading to throw the reading process out of focus. She takes into account that word recognition, for instance, is only one phase of reading and that it has no value without its proper relationship to the thought process vital to reading. If over-emphasis is given to it, word recognition not only fails to serve but distorts the development of reading. Gradually but surely each individual grows conscious of helpful techniques, such as seeing likenesses and differences in words or recognizing the use of capitals and periods. Always the children are reading. They are learning to read by reading, and techniques are learned as children practice them correctly in their reading. This argument denies the contention that the mastery of any one technique or set of techniques is a necessary requisite in the beginning stages of learning to read.

Manuscript writing is used with the beginning children in both their reading and writing because it more nearly resembles the symbols used in printing and so simplifies effort in both skills.

### Social Living Means More Reading

Social living involves a constant stream of communication. Reading and writing and spelling as such are lost in the process of communicating ideas, and letter writing becomes an exceedingly important social skill. In the spelling and writing aspects of communication, just as is true of the reading aspect, the children gradually take over more and more of the process. For example, a group of six-year-olds upon their return to school one morning found that Edgar had been in the room the evening before and had left the room in disorder. He was absent this day on account of illness. The group dictated while the teacher wrote the following letter:

February 26, 1941

Dear Edgar,

When we came to school this morning we found that you had left our room in an awful mess last night. You forgot to clean up before you left. The victrola records were on the table, and paper was cut up on the floor. Gladys had to clean up our room before school this morning. Miss Douthat has talked to you ever so many times about cleaning up. We do not like to go to a school that looks like people don't care about it.

We are sorry you could not come to school today. We miss you so much.

With love,<br>The boys and girls in<br>your room

Again a child may pick out a letter on the typewriter from a manuscript copy which he has dictated to the teacher:

Maury School

Dear mMother, I want you to
come from
        the hospital
    and bring little baby.
John

A third grade group on completing a piece of work which they had undertaken wrote and typed independently twenty different letters. Some of them follow:

Maury School
March 18, 1941

Dear Miss Fitzgerald,

We thank you for lending us your time in the playroom and I thank you for lending me your little velvet jacket.

From
Forest

Miss Fitzgerald is a teacher in Maury School.

Maury School
March 18, 1941

Dear Gladys,

I thank you for pressing
my costume.
I think you pressed it nice.
Thank you Gladys

Your friend
Hazel B

Gladys is a maid in Maury School.

Maury School
Richmond, Va.
March 18, 1941

Dear Miss Jones,

I thank you for the cup and the blue ribbon. I was proud to sit by C. W. Anderson with my riding pants and boots. And Mr. Anderson shook hands with me.

Love,
Billy

Miss Jones is a teacher in another Richmond school.

Maury School
March 18, 1941

Dear Miss Cole,

We want to thank you for letting Majorie come to Maury School to practice for our Book Fair play. I certainly did like the way that Majorie sang. She sang so sweet that the words looked like they were floating out of her mouth.

I hope that some time very soon we can come and help you all.

Jennie Rose

Miss Cole is a teacher in a neighboring school.

Typewriters easily accessible in classrooms enable children to communicate with others in a satisfactory way long before they have completely mastered writing techniques. They are able to manipulate the mechanical arrangement of the keyboard without laborious struggle at letter formation.

One of the problems to be continuously faced in this school where 450 people live together is a satisfactory handling of informal traffic. The narrow halls and hard floors make running a hazard. A common understanding is necessary. Teachers and children work continuously in dealing with the problem. Boys and girls representing each room met with one of the teachers one day to revise old plans and make new ones. These plans were recorded and distributed throughout the building:

CHILDREN WHO RUN MAY BE HURT.
ALWAYS REMEMBER TO WALK.
WALK ON THE RIGHT SIDE OF THE HALL.

The committee took the suggestions to each room and read them to the children who again discussed them. They were left in each room for all the children to use. There they were read again and again. Every child in school sensed the problems even before the committee met so that when the material came into the rooms everyone knew what it was even before he read it. Its vital, vivid content facilitated the reading process.

## The Enjoyment of Books Is Important

Another important feature of school life is the library. Everybody has a part in the selection of the books. A child, finding an interesting book at home or in the public library which he wishes added to the school library, brings a slip to the library noting the title, publisher and price of the book. This slip is placed on file and is considered for the regular school order at the proper time.

Enjoyment of books is a significant aspect of reading growth. Teachers spend much effort from the time the children enter school in reading beautiful books to them. Beautifully illustrated books of fine literary style are always available in the rooms for the children to use. Boys and girls speak with great familiarity of Lois Lenski, Munro Leaf and others. A new book by a favorite author brings great delight. Although the children read many books, dozens of them, they speak for their favorites and wait their turn, planning with the lucky children who get them first. In this they have the experience of shared enjoyment of books and of a common interest with book lovers. Sherwood, a third grade boy, made and illustrated a tiny book of which he was very proud and mailed it to Lois Lenski. He treasures her note of thanks. The morning he received it, he took it from person to person saying, "Not every child in Maury has a letter from Lois Lenski."

Living creatively with children while they have fine and appealing books around them has a direct influence on their writing. Reading, writing and spelling are constantly interrelated in rich experiences. One day Jimmie Thompson wrote and illustrated *The Little Red Cart*. The teacher took great pains to help him with the format of the book. His book had the same artistic qualities as the books purchased for the library. He took it to other rooms and children sat spellbound while he read it. Numbers of children keep this kind of free exchange of books in motion. Within a period of four months approximately one hundred books were made and interchanged between rooms. These books made by children became a part of the school library. Any time during the day one might see John reading the book he has made while three others listen in, or one might see the teacher helping Mary over difficult spots as she reads John's book.

## Recorded Experiences of Children

Recorded experiences of children constitute an important part of the little child's reading materials. Jean, a tiny girl in the beginning class, came to school one day wearing a new pair of beach shoes which all the children admired greatly and talked much about. Later in the day this chart appeared on the board:

PRETTY LITTLE SHOES!
THEY ARE RED AND BLUE.
WHAT FUN THEY WILL HAVE AT
THE BEACH THIS SUMMER!

It reechoed children's own words which they had forgotten they had said but which the teacher had mingled into interesting reading material. Throughout the morning Jean read the chart over and over and when her mother came at the close of the day she proudly walked over with her and read it to her.

Jane was laughing and talking on the rug one morning as the children struggled to get their snowsuits on. Later she saw her very own words on the reading chart. One child quickly pointed out that "You zip them" was exactly alike on the first two lines.

YOU ZIP THEM UP
YOU ZIP THEM DOWN
SNOWSUITS ARE HARD TO
GET INTO.

The children in Room 6 had a family of snails which they watched day by day. Several children were gathered around the jar one day talking as they watched. The chart reflected their conversation:

LOOK AT THAT ONE.
HE CLIMBED TO THE TOP.
POOR SNAIL!
HE FELL BACK DOWN.

Some quickly saw that "Look" and "Poor" each have two round letters in them. "Climbed" was easy because it was long and conspicuous and was the key word in the whole experience. While the children read the teacher constantly assists them in the proper use of reading mechanics, until they gradually develop independence in reading.

The teacher is constantly alert to children's conversations as the cue to reading material.

HERE COMES THE AMBULANCE!
SONNY MEYERS IS GETTING IN!
HE HAS ONLY A LITTLE CUT BUT
THE DOCTOR MUST SEE IT.

These are the children's words as they watched the ambulance taking Sonny to the hospital. He had fallen on the concrete walk and cut his face. The last lines reflect the teacher's effort to help them meet problems without excitement.

Sometimes the teacher finds expressions of real poetic quality. The children were standing by the window one day watching and talking as the snow was falling. This chart resulted:

SNOWFLAKES WHIRLING UP SO HIGH
THEY LOOK LIKE FEATHERS IN THE SKY.

James, a timid half-blind child, became adept at clay modeling. Everybody was trying to learn to mold figures without sticking on arms and legs. James amazed them one day with the man he made. He was excited because he had "squeezed it out of a lump." The chart that day read:

WHAT A NICE MAN!
HE WAS SQUEEZED OUT OF A LUMP.
FEEL HOW SOFT HE IS.

"Squeezed" was not a hard word for the children because the content of the story carried them over it. When the reading material for little children grows, as this did, out of their own lives, they approach it with eager anticipation. They know that something alive and interesting faces them every time they see a story.

One morning there was a new typewriter in Room 2. It had been loaned by a typewriter company. Of course everybody was eager to write his name. The teacher wrote the following chart:

CLICK, CLICK, CLICK!
COME AND WRITE YOUR NAME!
ANN, BILLY, MARIE, JOHN!
IT'S FUN TO TYPEWRITE.

The children were quick to notice the many capital letters. The teacher explained that they were used in names and at the beginning of sentences. The exclamation point interested them. She showed them how it was used to denote excitement or surprise.

Many, many such charts—hundreds of them representing the broad experiences of children—are brought into the room. An extensive and varied vocabulary, bound only by the limits of the child's experiences, is involved. As each chart comes into the room it is read for the meaning it conveys. When that is done, it has served its purpose and is put aside. The teacher is not interested in manipulating repetitive drill on words. She takes into account that the recurrence of words in rich and varied experiences, as they come and go, will in time fix a large vocabulary. Tabulation of the words used on charts in one room the first three months shows 350 words rather than the 60 found most commonly in the pre-primer type of reading materials.

Children do not all begin to master reading mechanics at the same age. Some begin at the age of six, some at seven and some even later. Many times the very bright child is not the first to begin reading. Sherwood, for instance, began to read at the opening of the third grade. At the close of the year, measured by group achievement tests, he tested in the middle of the fifth grade. The child who is slow in learning to read is provided the same rich experience that the other children enjoy. If he does not quickly master the mechanics of reading he is not singled out for drill in such isolated phases of reading as phonics and word drills. Instead he is given greater variety of beginner's materials extended over a longer period of time. This means, then, that the same fine quality in the reading processes is maintained for him even though it takes him a longer time to arrive at independence.

In directing a good reading program for little children the teacher's concern is with the scheme of day-by-day living which she and the children and the parents are continuously planning and revising. In such a setting of cooperative living, reading as a means of communication is constantly and abundantly present.

### Learning to Read Is a Personal Matter

Each child reading carries on a process which is both creative and unique. Reading has never been done before just as he does it nor will it ever be done just that way again. The child reading is thus the creator of his own reading process. Not only is the process not alike for any two children but it may not be the same with any one child on consecutive days.

Let us then consider individual children learning to read.

Thomas' world is influenced and dominated by a maiden aunt, a grandmother and a widowed mother. The aunt, who teaches English in high school, says she reads Browning and Tennyson for her own leisure reading and she hopes that Thomas will do the same. By the time Thomas entered school she had set up a library of books for him far in advance of his interest and years. "Some day," she says, "you will love and appreciate these beautiful books which I am collecting for you." Before he entered school she often read to him from Arabian Nights and King Arthur, books she felt he ought to enjoy. Living thus, in a nonchildlike atmosphere, guided always toward adult standards, he had been robbed of experiences at his level that would have created an appetite for reading. He came to school under the pressure "to learn to read." Thomas' major problem then was not a reading problem. The school's first responsibility was to create for him a child's world and to release him to live with abandon in such a world.

In this child's world he would live intimately with many, many books created for little children. Out of his daily living with children, standards appropriate for children would evolve which he could accept for himself to live by. In Thomas' case the process of getting himself out of artificiality and establishing his own real standards delayed the reading process. This delay was furthered by the adults in his family who, by constantly projecting their standards, created conflict for Thomas. When standards which were his own had been stabilized and he felt power in achieving them, he then began to teach himself to read.

Consider how different is the case of Malcolm. He, too, as an only child lived in an adult world surrounded by books. In his case, however, the setting was different. He had a fine library of the loveliest children's books, well suited to his tastes and needs. Because he was often sick, his mother constantly read and re-read his favorites to him. His home adjoined the city library and, from his earliest days, the children's librarians petted him and tried on him their new books before they were put on the shelves. He had travelled extensively and lived and talked with intelligent people. Again, as in Thomas' case, the school's major problem was not teaching Malcolm to read.

He had had many and varied experiences in books but a limited number of actual experiences with children of his own age. The school accepted the responsibility of emphasizing for him opportunities for work with groups of children in dramatizing, music, painting, clay modeling, outdoor play and all such childlike experiences. The school felt little concern that Malcolm showed no particular interest in mastery of reading techniques. Near the close of the second year he began to read and to read well. Apparently the school had not "taught" Malcolm to read but because reading was an inherent part of the process of school living, this growth had occurred.

Sylvester, a so-called mentally slow child, had his own special approach to reading. When he entered school he cried and clung to his mother. He had never left her in his life. At last, left alone at school, he sat and sobbed and sobbed; when anyone came close to him, he shrieked. He rarely smiled and never laughed with the other children. With this kind of beginning he was slow to take hold of anything. All through his first years of school life the teacher tried to build security for him and to help him make himself a place in the group. Not until the third year did Sylvester show any sign of a reading consciousness. Boys and girls in his class at this time had written and illustrated many interesting books. One day a significant happening occurred in Sylvester's life. He wrote and illustrated a book which he named *The Old Man Who Had Lots of Pets*. It took him a long time to write it. Effort was laborious. He read and reread the story many times but, from that time on, reading had significance for Sylvester. He read other children's books, for had they not read and liked his sad story of the old man and his pets? He had experienced success and so to the end of the year one book after another "flowed" from Sylvester's pencil. As he wrote he became interested in books and thus he began to read.

Kent in the third year was beginning to feel keenly conscious that he was being shut out of an alluring world of books which some of his best friends were entering. He sat and listened while they read to him. He saw child after child join the group reading books from the library. One day his best friend sat beside him and read from beginning to end *The Five Chinese Brothers.* When Harry finished, Kent clung to the book trying to read it. He kept his friend with him getting help on words for page after page. Harry finally left with the remarks, "Kent, I'm tired now." But Kent kept working, getting help from the teacher and from any child who would give it. In this, as in every case, the sincere desire to read is the force or compelling power which drives one forward.

Anne read *The Little Auto, Little Baby Ann* and *The Little White Teddy Bear.* When she finished a book she selected another of the same type and difficulty. In contrast to her way of working, when Jane finished *Ask Mr. Bear,* she selected and read *Babette.* Anne continuously read "easy" material but Jane selected progressively more difficult material. One day Jane was reading *Babette* with the teacher while Anne looked over her shoulder and enjoyed the book with her. Jane hesitated over a word and before the teacher could help her, Anne had supplied it. Personal selection of reading material is important in promoting growth and every individual should have opportunity to exercise choice. One child advances smoothly and gradually while another moves forward by spurts. There is no value in establishing a universal pattern for reading growth and, indeed, no real possibility of doing so.

Bobby in the second grade selected *Sharp Ears* to read. The difficulty of this book was apparently much above his reading

level but, intrigued by the content, he held to it. He followed
the whale from the Atlantic to the Pacific, getting words he
had never called before. No mechanical attack helped him here
but the creative thought process carried him somehow successfully over all difficulties.

William was a fine boy from an unfortunate home. In the
first grade he saw his portrait painted by one of his classmates
to decorate a reading chart. The chart read:

> WILLIAM IS OUR BANKER.
> HE KEEPS OUR MONEY.
> HE GIVES IT TO US AT LUNCHTIME.

A feeling for the content enabled William to participate with
the teacher in reading it, although his name was probably the
only word he recognized. Months passed and he participated
with interest in the same way in reading many other charts on
which his name occurred, such as:

> WHO SAW WILLIAM AT THE FAIR YESTERDAY?
> HE RODE THE CATERPILLAR.
> ARE YOU GOING TO THE FAIR?
>
> WE WENT TO SEE BETTY LOU IN GRACE
> HOSPITAL.
> SHE HAD HER APPENDIX TAKEN OUT.
> WILLIAM TOOK THE FLOWERS.

Always when his name appeared he was drawn to the chart and
was able to read it, although he read little else. But one day
when he was in the second grade he read with little assistance
the following chart:

> THURSDAY IS TURKEY DAY.
> MOTHERS AND FATHERS ARE INVITED.
> WILL YOUR MOTHER AND FATHER EAT LUNCH
> WITH YOU?

For months after this his reading was rough and irregular but
he did read. Growth was gradually and surely taking place.
Smooth performance was a long time coming. This was William's way of learning to read.

On entering school Lila was a keen, bright, mentally alert
child. Every interesting possibility for expression in the school
was a challenge to her. She painted enthusiastically; she danced
with abandon; she promoted dramatization; she made up thrilling stories and held the children spellbound with many dramatic gestures and on-the-spot interpolations. One day she sat
facing the group telling this story:

> *"Once there was a man, a farmer man. He had many chickens*
> *and ducks. He had four children, too. He lived in the country*
> *a long ways from the city. One day he told his children to go out*
> *doors and see what the ducks were doing. He kept his ducks in*
> *the barn in the yard."* (At this moment a very personable
> gentleman with a moustache enters the back of the room.)
> *"I forgot to tell you the farmer had a teeny, tiny moustache in*
> *the middle of his top lip."*

Reading was only one of Lila's many and varied interests,
not the exclusive interest in her life. At her own good time
she began to read. Every child, if reading is to be a successful
experience, must so make his own natural integration and nice
balance of relationships.

Reading is a human being's reaction to life about him. With
thirty children in a room, there may be thirty different approaches to reading and need, therefore, for thirty kinds of
guidance. There may be thirty different individual rates of
progress. The teacher's concern must be to understand the
unique characteristics of each child in order that she may assist
in maintaining quality in effort, for it is the quality in effort
that is significant.

## The Kind and Quality of Material Has
## an Important Bearing on Reading

Maury School books are picturesque, exciting, colorful, beautiful. The school physician on his way to his office in the school stopped and thumbed through the D'Aulaires beautiful *Abraham Lincoln*. Mothers passing in and out of the building have remained at children's tables to read a book. James waited for days for his turn at *Robert Francis Weatherbee* because his grandmother had asked him to bring it home for her to read. *Madeline* went into home after home upon requests from parents. Once one copy of *The Story of Horace* was in a room being read to the five-and-a-half year olds. The next day Hunter in the third grade was reading it to himself and others, and the following day Mrs. Cox borrowed it in order that Mr. Cox might read it. So books travel from room to room and in and out of homes.

There are no first grade books. There are no third grade books. The Maury School library is available to every child in the building. The selection of books goes on continuously. Any teacher, parent or child who runs across a good book feels it his responsibility to place it on the ordering list. There are no text books as such. No sets of books are ordered for group reading. *I Know a Story* is there because children like it. *Through the Year, The Find Out Book,* and all other good text books are there because at certain times they exactly fit the needs of individual children. The library shelves are lined with carefully selected books appealing to every type of interest.

No dividing lines are set up between books for information and books for pleasure. Just before Christmas Margaret definitely sought out *Art Stories* for very specific information regarding the painting of Madonnas. She was at work on a picture to be used as a decoration for Christmas. Jean, on the other hand, read the whole series more than once because she is interested in all types of art and all types of color. Dick, one very cold day, put the thermometer outside the window to test the difference in temperature indoors and out. Immediately he looked for one of the Craig books on science for specific information about using the thermometer. Charlie, who is very curious about the world around him, likes no books for pleasure reading better than this type. Any good book may be used one moment by a child in search of information, the next moment for sheer pleasure. Moreover, any number of books that have been classified as books for pure pleasure reading are rich in informational content. For illustration, the delightful nonsense in *The Story Dr. Doolittle* presents vivid pictures of the English countryside and of the tropical jungles. *Mike Mulligan and his Steam Shovel* helps the child to interpret and to understand the workings of the machine age in which he lives. In *The Story of Ping* the child's understanding of life on the river boats of China is enlarged. *Blue Willow* carries the child along in the charm of its narrative but, at the same time, it gives insight into one of today's social problems.

Maury School books are children's familiar and well-loved friends. John brought a caterpillar into the room one morning. Instantly Dolores said, "Wait a minute, I'll find the page about the caterpillar," and she opened *Let's Go Outdoors*. Julia showed the children a spray of Queen Anne's Lace. No sooner had she done this than Margaret and Jacqueline were at the book case. Margaret returned with a science book picturing a field of Queen Anne's Lace and giving information about it which she offered to read to the children. Jacqueline had picked up *Silver Pennies* and asked to read the poem about Queen Anne's Lace. No less familiar are they with authors and illustrators and the making of books. Joyce Ann, examining a book she had never seen before, brought it to the teacher and said, "This book was born the same year I was."

The reading material that appeals to children is that which appeals to their imagination, enlarges their experiences and reflects their own language. For illustration, a group of seven-year-olds read intelligently the following material:

> DIDN'T WE HAVE A GOOD TIME IN ASSEMBLY THIS MORNING?
> CHARLIE McCARTHY WAS SO FUNNY!
> HE WILL BE AT THE CARNIVAL.

One might say this contains "hard" words and a long sentence. As a matter of fact children rapidly got "Charlie McCarthy," "assembly," and "carnival." While this might look to be an isolated paragraph, it is really a segment of the child's life and has meaning to him because he knew what came before and he knows what is coming afterwards. It is, therefore, not a thing in itself. Many books that have been considered easy for beginners are in reality hard books. For instance, those lines from one of the usual books: *Kitty Cat washed herself. She washed herself clean. Kitty Cat is a clean cat.* This material in contrast to the above, while it contains only eight different words, is "hard." While it may be true that children have seen cats wash and under certain conditions would be interested in seeing a specific cat wash, this is a generalized cat and, as such, is of no special interest to children; nor are the ideas expressed in language that children would use. This type of material, made in an effort to simplify the vocabulary for slow readers, has often been recommended as good. We have not found it so. When Tommy, a reader of this type, was given an opportunity to select from books built on such a vocabulary his comment was, "Just don't show me any of that stuff."

Easy-to-read material is not produced by limiting the vocabulary or by omitting colorful, picturesque, exciting words. These make material easy. Isolated paragraphs like the one above about Charlie McCarthy are easy and interesting to the particular group for which they have meaning. They do not have universal appeal. Stories that are simply told and are complete in themselves such as *The Gingerbread Boy, Three Bears* and *Little Red Riding Hood* are "easy" for children to read. The content, the style that kindles the imagination and sets free creative thought, makes reading material easy. *The Little Auto, Robert Francis Weatherbee, The Little Teddy Bear,* and many others like them are easy for children for this reason.

When children write their own stories and books, these reflect the type of material they really like and can really use to advantage. First of all these books tell a story and are complete in themselves, however simple they may be. To illustrate:

### Page 1

*Once there was an old man.*
*He had thirty dogs.*
(A crude drawing at the bottom of the page shows a house with a fence around it. A dog and man are seen inside the fence.)

### Page 2

*Four of them died.*
(Four graves, each with flowers and a cross on it, crudely drawn at the bottom of the page.)

### Page 3

*Three of them were sick.*
(Three beds in a row, with a dog in each, crudely drawn at the bottom of the page.)

## Page 4

*The man had two chickens, three hens, and four cows.*
*He had a big old German police dog.*
(The house with two chickens and a big dog in front of it, crudely drawn at the bottom of the page.)

## Page 5

*The old man had blood poison and died.*
(A huge grave with flowers and a cross crudely drawn at the bottom of the page.)

## Page 6

*The dog dug a big hole and buried him.*
(The dog sniffing at the hole crudely drawn at the bottom of the page.)

## Page 7

*The dog took care of the chickens and cows.*
(The dog standing by the house crudely drawn at the bottom of the page.)

## Page 8

*A little boy came by one day. When he saw that the old man was not there he came in the house and took care of them. They lived happily ever after.*
(A big house with a boy in front of it.)

Consider also this story by a third-grade girl:

## Page 1

*Once upon a time there lived a little girl named Beatrice. She was a cute little girl but her disposition wasn't very nice. One day a little girl named Joan came to see her. Beatrice wouldn't share her toys with Joan so Joan went home.*
(A picture of Joan and Beatrice.)

INDIVIDUALIZED READING IN ACTION

## Page 2

*That night after Beatrice had gone to bed a little man came in the window of her room and said "Come with me." "I'll have to dress," said Beatrice. "I'll wait," said the little man. So Beatrice dressed and went with the little man. "Get on my back and we will be ready to go."*

(Beatrice asleep. A little man with wings peeping in the window.)

## Page 3

*"But you are so small. I'll attend to that," he said. All of a sudden Beatrice began to grow smaller and smaller until she was no bigger than the little man himself! Beatrice was a little afraid but she did not want the little man to know it, so she smiled and went with him.*

(Beatrice and the little man standing by a chair. They reach to the seat.)

## Page 4

*He took her far over house tops until he stopped in front of a great castle. There he put Beatrice down on the ground and said, "Followyournose Whereveritgoes." Beatrice went from room to room. Soon she came to a big room that was filled with children.*

(The little man with Beatrice on his back flying over houses.)

## Page 5

*Some children had toys and some did not. The ones that had toys were sharing theirs with those who didn't have any. Beatrice hung her head in shame. She called the little man so he could take her back home. The little man said, "Get on my back and I will take you back home."*

(Two little girls and a toy wagon.)

## Page 6

*As Beatrice got into her bed she felt herself growing larger and larger but she didn't worry about it. She was too sleepy.*

*The next morning after Beatrice had eaten her breakfast, Joan
came back to visit.*
(Beatrice lying in her bed. Stars seen through the window.)

### Page 7

*To her mother's surprise Beatrice asked Joan what she wanted
to play. Joan said she wanted to play* Mama and Children, *one
of the things that Beatrice did* NOT *like to play. But today
Beatrice said, "All right."*
(Beatrice's head, "All right" coming from her mouth.)

### Page 8

*After Joan had gone home Beatrice's mother asked her what
had come over her. Beatrice said, "Nothing." She never told
her mother what had happened*

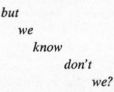

   *but*
      *we*
         *know*
            *don't*
              *we?*

In these books we see the efforts of the very beginners in
reading and story-writing (*The Old Man Who Had Lots of
Pets*), as well as that of the third grade girl whose book *The
Changed Girl* has unusual form and content. All of these are
interesting to children because they tell something that children
want to read about and in a style which appeals to them.

These books which they write show the impression of good
books which they have read and enjoyed. For instance the end-
ing of *Bran and Tan* is definitely reminiscent of *Little Black
Sambo:* "*They went home and had coconuts, bananas, and all
kinds of fruit. Even sugar cane! Tan and Bran ate more than
two hundred sugar canes apiece.*" *The King's Duck* is a child's
story of a magic duck who could put out fires and know what

witches were thinking. It has some of the characteristics of *Drakesbill*. The very stuff of *Twin Red Stilts* is the author walking on the playground on stilts that had been newly painted red and are especially popular with all the children. The opening paragraph reveals something of its contents: *"Once upon a time there were twin red stilts. The twin red stilts were unhappy. They were coming loose. The little boy walked on them too hard."* In true "Andersen style" Jackie has made inanimate objects talk and act in character and the readers' sympathies are with the twin red stilts. *The Little Princess Who Tore Her Dress* is pure fancy. The little princess is in sore distress because she has torn her dress on a rose bush and a fairy god-mother appears to help her out of her difficulty, just as so many fairies have appeared in fairy tales all through the ages.

The picturesque titles which children gave their characters —*Bumpy Alligator, Whoopty Doopty, Mr. Croak, Mrs. Tippentopper,* or *Mr. Button Popper*—show that their experiences with reading have been varied and vivid.

Books constitute a vital part of the environment. Reading a book is a high adventure. When children have lived always with books that have meaning and challenge to them they approach each new experience with expectancy, zest, and curiosity. Reading is thrilling.

*Five Chinese Brothers,* Bishop, C. H. Coward-McCann, 1938.
*Little Auto,* Lois Lenski, Oxford, 1934.
*Little Baby Ann,* Lois Lenski, Oxford, 1935.
*Little Teddy Bear,* Eliott, L. S. Collins, 1939.
*Ask Mr. Bear,* Flack, M., Macmillan, 1932.
*Babette,* Newberry, C. I. Harper, 1937.
*Sharp Ears, The Baby Animal,* J. L. Beaty, Lippincott, 1938.
*Abraham Lincoln,* D'Aulaires, Doubleday, 1939.
*Robert Francis Weatherbee,* Munro Leaf, Chattel, 1938.

*Madeline,* Bemelmans, L. Simon and Schuster, 1939.

*Story of Horace Coats,* A. M. Ryerson Press, 1939.

*I Know a Story,* Huber, M. B. Row Peterson, 1938.

*Through the Year,* Frazier, G. W. Singer.

*The Find Out Book,* University of North Carolina. Compiled by first grade teachers of Orange City, Mary W. Hyman, Supervisor.

*Art Stories,* Whitford, W. C. Reilly & Co.

*The Story of Dr. Doolittle,* Lofting H., Stokes, 1920.

*Mike Mulligan and His Steam Shovel,* Burton, V. L., Houghton, 1939.

*Story of Ping,* M. Flack, Viking, 1933.

*Blue Willow,* Gates D., Viking, 1940.

*Let's Go Outdoors,* Huntington, H. E., Doubleday, 1939.

*Silver Pennies,* Thompson, B. J. ed., Macmillan, 1925.

*Little Black Sambo,* Bannerman, H., Stokes, 1923.

| Chapter | SEEKING, SELF-SELECTION, AND |
| 2. | PACING IN THE USE OF BOOKS BY CHILDREN |

## 2.

# SEEKING, SELF-SELECTION, AND PACING IN THE USE OF BOOKS BY CHILDREN

*Willard C. Olson,*
*Director of Research in Child Development,*
*University of Michigan.*

*In the years 1952-53 several significant pieces appeared that have given a major push to the concept of individualizing reading. Below is one of the most important of these significant contributions.*

THE RAPIDLY GROWING body of knowledge concerning the nature of growth, behavior, and achievement has numerous implications for practices in the schools. Three useful concepts emerge on the ways in which books may be used by children and teachers for purposes of problem solving, information, or entertainment and relaxation. They are seeking behavior, self-selection, and pacing.

## Seeking Behavior

The healthy child is naturally active and he is engaged almost continually while awake in an active exploration of his environment. He seeks from that environment those experiences that are consistent with his maturity and his needs. Other aspects, even though present, are ignored, for he does not react to

*Packet,* Spring, 1952, Vol. 7, No. 1. This is a further treatment of material originally presented in Dr. Olson's book *Child Development,* D. C. Heath Co., Boston, 1949. Used by permission of the publisher.

them and therefore does not learn appreciably from them. Since children grow at widely varying rates, it is impossible to say that they will be ready for a particular experience at a specific age. We can, however, trust the seeking behavior to tell us much about the readiness of a child for an experience. This is evident even in the first year of life as the child begins to understand, later as he begins to talk, and in his early responsiveness to pictured materials found in the home. The longer the children have an opportunity to grow and the more experiences that they have, the more different do they become and the less ready are they for a common experience—either in terms of difficulty level or in terms of interests. How does one in practice use the seeking tendencies of children to advance their competence in skills, attitudes, and information? Here, self-selection becomes a useful concept.

### Self-selection

Throughout nature there is a strong tendency for life to be sustained by the self-selection of an environment appropriate to the needs of the plant, animal, or human being. If the appropriate environment does not exist ready made or is inadequate in some major respects, the human being also works creatively for the conditions that advance his well being. Investigations show that infants have great ability to regulate the amount and timing of their food intake to harmonize (wtih) their needs, and that they accept and reject foods on the basis of flavors, consistency, or quantity, in ways appropriate to their maturity.

We do not, however, need to borrow from other fields of investigation to illustrate how teachers may use the principle of self-selection as a means for bringing together the nurturing qualities in books with the seeking tendencies of children.

If young children in the preschool period are turned loose in an environment in which there exists a variety of stimulating objects, each child will tend at appropriate times to react to some of the material but he will react differentially according to the rapidity with which he is maturing. Thus, in such an environment, the more mature child will spend more time with books while, for a period, such materials will be ignored by the less mature child—even though he is of equal age.

Refinements in the psychology of reading and in the technology of book construction now make it possible for even the slowly growing child to have a more successful first experience as he seeks and reacts to reading materials in a spontaneous way or because the teacher places it before him with deliberate intent to secure a response. The most artistic and scientific teacher is the one who is a close observer and ensures the simpler transitional experiences needed by the less mature. A less professional teacher tries to secure uniform responses to uniform materials—but never with success. If humanely attempted there may be no permanent dulling of the child's seeking behavior by efforts to secure responses for which a child is unready, but there appear to be instances where the social and emotional repercussions in the child and the family illustrate the danger of introducing such basic frustrations into the life of a child. When a teacher or parent has a high regard for seeking behavior and self-selection the child grows into the reading experience. With an accelerated child this happens so quickly that one can hardly understand the elements of the method. In slowly growing children the process is usually the same but much later. Some children in the third grade are still as immature as some in the kindergarten and first grade. If basic differences in the rate of growing up are not taken into account, the process may become painful to child, to parent, and to the teacher.

A brief summary of a classroom experiment in a second grade will illustrate the meaning of the concept of self-selection.

The teacher, the school librarian, and the children cooperated in developing a room library which contained 115 titles of readers and stories from pre-primer to fourth grade level and represented many interests.

No assignments were made by the teacher, but she remained an encouraging guide and often was a part of an appreciative audience. Experience reading continued as a part of the program. The adjustment to individual differences was made by allowing the children to browse and sample in the room library and select those books that they wished to read.

The results can be indicated briefly by the accompanying illustration. Bill read 21 books and gained 19 months in reading age during the seven months of the study, as indicated by the solid lines.

John read 13 books and gained 12 months in reading age during the period of the experiment. This was the average result for the group.

James read four books during the study and made no measurable gain on the test used.

James's slow growth in reading was not a consequence of the small number of books read. His behavior toward reading was rather a symptom of his general immaturity. Teachers before, during, and after the experiment had brought their best skill to bear on the improvement of his reading. Time and maturation were necessary to bring about a spurt. James at 13 and 14 finally achieved a status in reading somewhat above his chronological age.

This type of late spurt for children who start slowly happens often enough to be reassuring to those who are inclined to worry too much about the child who does not stand out in the early grades.

With the power gained in the second grade the children in

the illustration went on into the third grade, where Bill read 110 books, John 123, and James 12.

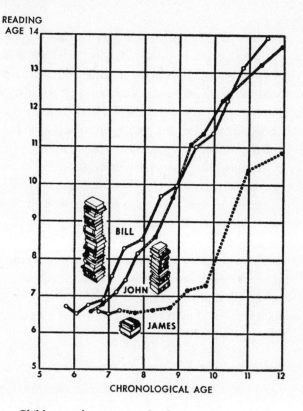

*Children seek nurture in books according to their
level and rate of growth.*

One cannot, of course, understand completely what is behind the relative rates of growth shown in the curves for reading without also studying the same children from the point of view of the child as a whole. This more comprehensive study— including measures of height and weight, strength, intelligence, ossification of wrist bones, eruption of the teeth, and much social and emotional data—has been made. John and Bill were advanced in these measures while James was slow.

## Pacing

Pacing refers to the acts on the part of the teacher which ensure that each child is provided with the materials upon which he can thrive and also to the attitude which expects from the child only that which he can yield at his stage of maturity. Just as the concept of self-selection has back of it a psychology of motivation, so also does the pacing approach have back of it concepts of the nature of success, incentive, and productivity. Studies of learning and productivity in relationship to the goals that are set suggest that the child will continue to strive when success is clearly within his grasp. He will start avoiding the experiences which are at a level of difficulty clearly beyond his present attainments. The teacher's task is to guarantee that every classroom situation, or its immediate surroundings, will have in it tasks which are interesting in terms of the intrinsic content, and which also cover a range of difficulty as great as the variability in the human material with which he deals. How is this to be accomplished?

## The Self-selection Packet and Room Library

A teacher who is interested in trying out seeking, self-selection, and pacing concepts in reading might well begin with a self-selection packet as a nucleus of a room library. The self-selection packet can be preplanned in terms of the variability in reading commonly found in each grade. This variability will be altered somewhat by the promotion policies of a school but no plan for classification or teaching has successfully eliminated individual differences, given homogeneous groups, or made important differences in the fundamental rates of growing.

Self-selection from a large supply, such as a children's library, is a dynamic way for children, the librarian, and a teacher to participate in setting up a room library. In most situations, however, budgets must be planned economically, books may not be physically accessible, and there must be some pre-planning in requisitions. If one becomes really in earnest about supplying books at a range of difficulty and interest level to meet the individual differences of all children, he will find the figures in the Table which follows of interest and of assistance.

The Table is very approximate and is set up with certain assumptions in mind. The ages taken as representative of the

### THE PERCENTAGE OF CHILDREN IN EACH GRADE READY FOR EACH BOOK LEVEL

| Book Level | | Grade Level | | | | | |
|---|---|---|---|---|---|---|---|
| GRADE | AGE | I | II | III | IV | V | VI |
| N.S. | 5 | 2 | 2 | 2 | | | |
| Kg. | 6 | 23 | 8 | 5 | 7 | | |
| 1 | 7 | 50 | 24 | 11 | 9 | 7 | |
| 2 | 8 | 23 | 33 | 20 | 10 | 9 | 7 |
| 3 | 9 | 2 | 24 | 24 | 16 | 10 | 9 |
| 4 | 10 | | 8 | 20 | 17 | 16 | 10 |
| 5 | 11 | | 2 | 11 | 16 | 17 | 16 |
| 6 | 12 | | | 5 | 10 | 16 | 17 |
| 7 | 13 | | | 2 | 9 | 10 | 16 |
| 8 | 14 | | | | 7 | 9 | 10 |
| 9 | 15 | | | | | 7 | 9 |
| 10 | 16 | | | | | | 7 |

grades are based on an entrance policy by which children must be at least five years of age upon entrance to the kindergarten, calculated as of September 1. That means that the entering class will range from five up to six and will average five and one half, and on March 1 will average six. Similarly, the other values are March 1 dates. The Table is also constructed on the idea that most of the children are to be promoted each year.

Variations from the above assumptions do not change the children but would change the statistics in minor details.

The Table can be interpreted as follows: Looking under grade one at the top, and opposite grade one on the side, it can be determined that fifty per cent of the children will be working at the grade one level and will be approximately age seven in ability as of March 1. However, twenty-three per cent will be at the kindergarten level and two per cent will be at the nursery school level. On the other hand, twenty-three per cent will be at the second grade level and two per cent will be at the third grade level. At no time in their history will the children ever be so homogeneous again. By the time the second grade is reached, there will be only thirty-three per cent at the modal age for the grade. The others will be distributed on each side from nursery school level to an occasional one at the fifth grade level. The longer children are exposed to the opportunity to learn to read, the more different they become. By the time the sixth grade is reached, only seventeen per cent are right at the sixth grade level. Almost as many are at fifth and seventh grade levels and they vary from that for an eight-year range from eight to sixteen as shown in the Table. Actually, the range in all of the grades is slightly wider than shown. Is it surprising that teachers have had headaches when they have tried to teach a particular grade as if there were in it constant human material?

At one time, it was thought that a solution would lie in retaining the slow readers. For example, if one were to send or hold back thirty-four per cent of the second grade children, those that remained in that grade would be at second grade level and above. Similarly eighteen per cent of the third, sixteen per cent of the fourth and seven per cent of the fifth would need to be kept in the first grade and additional numbers retained one or more years. Such heroic measures create more problems than they solve, since the consequences of retention, failure, and repeated failure are dangerous.

When one turns to the idea that it is the task of the school to teach children rather than grades, some simplifications occur. Each grade then could have approximately the range of difficulty of materials indicated by the Table and the possibilities of every child being successful at his level of growth would be enhanced. So far as we now know, the differences shown in the Table are not likely to be ironed out by an improvement in either books or teaching method. Until research points the way to something better than we have now it appears to be the part of wisdom to accept variability as a fact, to be skillful in meeting it, and to be happy in the thought that every child can grow.

If a teacher wishes to have one book in the hands of each child, the percentages in the Table would be a rough guide to purchases. Such a provision, however, could only be regarded as a beginning core because the children at the different levels consume books at rates which differ widely. Thus, in grade two, it is probable that the most rapidly growing children would read five times as many books as the least rapidly growing children. The statistics on self-selection are not sufficiently well known to give reliable figures for the differential rates of consumption of books. After power has been attained it is also possible for a given child to read materials over a range of difficulty. Some books, although very simple, are still interesting, and others which require a child to stretch are challenging.

The teacher will find it of great assistance to use the carefully graded and studied materials produced by leading textbook authors and publishers in setting up the core for the self-selection packet or room library. The presence of such materials will assist in a graded introduction and supply a sequence. Some children will consume a few and some many books in such a progression during the course of the year. Such materials also can be selected so as to contain a probable appeal to the varying interests that are found in a classroom group. In addition, however, children should have access to a further supply of children's literature and reference materials from which they will exercise selection for the room library so as to elaborate special interests or to find materials in greater quantity as they become prolific readers. No very good statistics are available on the breadth that would be needed. In one study in a second grade, over one hundred books were utilized in such a library in a period of seven months. A fifth grade group, exploiting a large children's library, utilized over 500 titles.

It is clear that the provision of a lush environment of books related to the varying rates of growth and interests of children contemplates an expenditure substantially larger than has been customary in elementary education. There may be practical limitations, but no scientific justification for the educational deprivation which occurs under some narrow interpretations of the nature of the reading process and of its value in the whole educational enterprise.

To help children to grow, we should take each child where he is and provide him with and allow him to seek appropriate experiences under social conditions which also maintain his eagerness, his zest, his confidence, and his pride in successful achievement at his level.

# INDIVIDUALIZING READING

*Frances Maib,*
*Associate Professor of Elementary Education,*
*University of Idaho*

*This article contributed another significant push in the direction of the individualization of the teaching of reading. The practical, concise and enthusiastic description of an emerging practice found interested readers on the national scene. Many teachers, supervisors and administrators, now discovered they were not alone in departing from traditional ability grouped methods. A nation-wide community of interest was beginning to develop.*

RECENTLY, THE WRITER observed a fourth grade reading group of about fifteen students. During the period of approximately twenty-five minutes, nonparticipating individuals awaiting their "turn," lost interest, and in some cases sought diversion. This lack of interest was particularly evident when some poor reader stumbled slowly over the story. It can be said that each member of that group wasted about twenty-three minutes. The only individual gain was found in the approximately two minutes' time when the child's "turn" came to read. In addition to this waste of time, a lack of interest developed, some unsocial habit patterns were formed, and, in some cases, reading speed may actually have been decreased. In general, maximum individual efficiency was not reached.

From *Elementary English,* February 1952. Reprinted by permission of the author and the publishers of *Elementary English.*

This is a situation unfortunately common in teaching experience. For years, educators have understood the concept of individual levels of ability existent among the students in every schoolroom, and in the search for a method to meet these individual differences, teachers quite universally concluded that regimented instruction had failed. A more satisfactory approach was needed, one which would allow for the variations in individual status, growth patterns, physical and mental endowments, past experiences, hopes, desires, and other background factors which make up a child's ability.

## Grouping as a Solution

As one answer to the need, the method of "grouping" classes became popular. This was an attempt to adapt the work more adequately to the ability level of the students. However, the alert teacher soon discovered that even with this concession, there was still such a range of ability that only the average student in any given group was being taught near the range of his maximum capacity. The more advanced students were not being challenged, and the more retarded children were having difficulty in keeping up with the work and in many instances were developing psychological problems, including emotional blockages. If the teacher were to recognize these individual differences it must be at the expense of other members of the group, awaiting their "turn."

In view of these difficulties, the group method, while an improvement on regimented instruction, was not a satisfactory solution. It was not meeting the needs of each child in the most efficient and economical manner. In addition, it tended to create a spirit of competition in which the children vie for status in the highest group, for, despite efforts to keep the rank of each group unknown, the children were adept in determining the ratings.

If these considerations are applied to the field of reading, it can be noted at once that authorities agree quite generally that success in this activity stimulates further effort and consequently additional success. On the contrary, failure breeds failure. If the child, even within a selected group, has his success measured by the ability of the group rather than by success in proportion to his individual ability, he may feel the sting of failure in his efforts to meet the standard of the group. And if he merely "follows the place" while other members are reading, he not only wastes time, but often slows his own reading speed by following the oral reading pace of another.

It is not the purpose of this article to be uncharitable toward the group method. Rather, the writer recognizes the contribution it has made and the stepping stone it has been to a more efficient technique: the individualized reading method.

## How Individualization Works

Individualized reading is just what the name implies. It is a method which enables the student to have a program adapted to his personal needs, with materials fitted to his reading ability, and the entire reading time devoted to his individual reading problems and interests.

In initiating an individualized reading program, the teacher should explain to the pupils that they are no longer reading in groups, but that each child will be choosing his own books, reading at his own speed, and studying his own word lists. Some children may read only a few pages in a given time while others may read several stories. Before the children become accustomed to the plan, they may do some superficial reading in an attempt to get a new book, and the teacher should be constantly alert for this contingency. Normally, however, this superficial reading will disappear as competition is minimized and personal interest develops. The teacher may check the efficiency of the reading being done by having the child read orally, tell a portion of the story, discuss a particular part, or pronounce selected words.

If a visitor should enter a third grade room just as the teacher under this plan tells the pupils it is time for reading, he will see each child getting out his own materials and starting to read silently in his own place. One or two students may be working on some phonics which the teacher has supplied to meet given needs. Several may be reading fourth grade books, one or two even a fifth grade book, while some will be reading on a lower level. One may be reviewing or studying his word list, others doing some creative work connected with what they have been reading, and some, who need help with words, may be getting assistance from a capable student (the value of this may be questioned by some teachers, and should be used only at the discretion of the individual teacher).

The teacher, meanwhile, will be working individually, as needed, with the students. This individual help will include judgment as to whether the children have a genuine interest in their reading, stimulation and encouragement where needed, a shared enjoyment of stories with the children, provision of frequent opportunity for the pupils to read orally, individual drill on difficult words, and assistance in the choice of a new book when the child is ready for it. At first glance this may seem an impossible task, but the teacher will soon discover that with this individual plan she can devote as much time as before to each student, the main difference being that the other members of the class are going ahead with their own reading instead of waiting for a "turn," or being drilled on words they already know.

For those who feel that under this plan the child is too much on his own, it should be noted that if the approximate amount of time per day for reading is sixty minutes, with four minutes given to an individual student (which is easily equal to the amount of personal time he would receive under the group method), fifteen children could have their needs met daily. This number could be increased if, in the teacher's judgment, an adjustment should be made in the distribution of time.

Under this plan several approaches may be made to word study. Perhaps the most successful is use of an individual word list which the child keeps as he reads, and to which the teacher adds as difficulties arise. Some children enjoy a "word basket," in which they keep old words needing additional study, together with the new words they are meeting. The amount of time given to word study and to oral reading will vary from daily drill for those who have the greatest need, to an occasional recitation for the more apt children. The teacher should, however, take care that there is a reasonable distribution of time among all students.

### Individualized Reading Materials

The reading material needed for this work will be supplied by selection from the many textbooks which are published by reliable companies. In addition to books on the grade level of the class, there should also be some on other grade levels. For example, in the fourth grade, there would be many fourth grade texts, but also numerous books ranging from first to sixth grades. If, however, this plan for reading is not followed throughout the school, teachers should be careful not to use basic texts from more advanced grades. On the other hand, if all the teachers adhere to this method, no difficulty will occur because the child will continue his progress where he left off in the preceding grade. In many communities where schools are faced with a possible dearth of reading materials, there are circulating state and county libraries which could fill existing needs.

If the teacher feels that opportunities for social development cannot be adequately supplied in other learning activities, she may wish to plan for an occasional period when children share their reading experience. Some teachers use the children's weekly newspapers for this, or the children may prefer to read aloud to the group an interesting paragraph or portion of a story. In some rooms where an informal atmosphere exists, the children may go in groups of two or three and read to each other just for the enjoyment of sharing. Sometimes they may wish to sit near friends while each reads his own material, and if one needs help, his friends are there to offer it.

The question may arise as to the size of class in which this program can be used successfully. Actually, size is not important; it is, indeed, easier to use individualized reading in a large class than to use the group method. In a group of twelve, for example, while the teacher is meeting the needs of one child, the other eleven members of the group are frequently wasting time. Therefore, it requires no more time, and is certainly more efficient, to work with each child individually while the other children are constructively occupied, than to work with individual problems when the children are in a group.

Some may doubt the applicability of this method in the first grade, where there is no reading vocabulary or background, but it is actually most effective here. Reading is a particularly difficult subject to teach by the group method at this level because the pupils' abilities and stages of development are so varied. Therefore, if children can be taught beginning reading individually by the method best suited to their needs and abilities, most of the reading problems which normally develop will be eliminated. Teachers quite generally agree that a child should start to read when he shows the readiness for it, and the individualized method offers unusual opportunities to meet this condition. The writer has discussed the values of this method with first grade teachers who have used it, and they are of the opinion that individualized reading is the answer to most of their reading problems. These first grade teachers constitute just as enthusiastic a group in favor of this method as do the teachers at other levels.

## Individualization Gets Results

One of the advantages of individualized reading over other methods is the elimination of pressure and tension from the student in his attempt to meet the standards of his group. Why should he be compared with anyone else? He is not exactly like anyone else. When group competition is removed and the child is allowed to compete against himself, his own ability becomes the standard by which he is judged and tensions and pressures will give way to a more relaxed and more efficient type of study. The removal of this pressure should also eliminate the development of possible emotional blockages and undesirable attitudes toward reading.

Maximum efficiency in the use of a child's time is another advantage of individualized reading. The student does not drill with a group on words which only certain members in the group do not know. Instead, he spends time only on his own list of words *he* does not know. The amount of time which the student spends in silent reading is also increased because he need not wait while others are reading orally. Instead, he spends his time in doing his own silent reading or in activities related to this reading.

The psychological effect of individual reading is excellent. The slow reader is getting results and the fast reader is enjoying his reading. No stigma is felt about what is read or the amount read. Indeed, in one instance one of the slow readers finished a book that a fast reader had not read yet. Because the faster reader had missed the book and knew there were good stories in it, he asked for it. He had learned to read for enjoyment and felt no embarrassment about reading a book which a poorer reader had just finished.

Acceleration in reading speed is a natural consequence of covering large quantities of material which is on the interest and ability level of the student. This method provides unequaled opportunity for such coverage, and there is no possibility of slowing the silent reading speed to that of the oral speed of students being "followed," as is often done in group work.

Reading interest is also stimulated and increased by individualized reading. Each child, besides being an individual, has individual ideas and tastes, which he should be allowed to pursue. It is natural for a child to be more interested in reading material adapted to his capacities and chosen by himself, than in that which he is scarcely able to read, or which is so simple for him that it may not offer him a challenge. It should be noted, however, that after a child has made his choice, under the teacher's direction he should be expected to read the entire book before taking another. Few exceptions should be made to this rule.

One third grade teacher, wishing to determine which method had greatest interest and was most popular with the students, used the individualized method for a given period, and then changed to the group method. Twice she followed this alternation, with convincing results. The children were bored with the group approach and emphatically insisted on going back to their own reading. When the teacher privately interviewed some of these children, and asked reasons for their preference, she received the following typical replies:

Boy—'Cause I don't have to wait for the others while they are reading. I don't have to read the same books as everyone else. I read my own stories.

Boy—I learn to read better.

Girl—I like to read by myself because it's just fun. You get more done.

Boy—Well, you can read longer and when the reading groups are over you can still be reading. Get more work done.

Girl—I can read better when I read to myself.

Girl—You get to read more books with better stories.

Boy—When you're in a group you know what's going to happen in the stories 'cause the kids tell, but they can't when you read by yourself. The stories are exciting.

Boy—In a reading class you miss words. You don't when you read by yourself. You read them all.

Girl—I don't like a group and my books are real good.

Girl—I like it because it's a pleasure and a hobby of mine to read alone.

Girl—When you are ready for a book you can have it. You don't have to wait for anyone else.

Boy—Don't have to stop and read in the middle of work.

Such testimonials convinced this teacher that individualized reading was most effectively meeting the desires and needs of the pupils.

Finally, this method results in consistently larger amounts of reading for the student. In one instance, children, on their own and free to read as opportunity permitted, read forty to eighty pages a day, as compared to ten or twelve pages in group reading, where most teachers require the students not to read ahead. In another instance, a third grade girl transferred in January to a school which used the individualized method. From the preceding September until January, when she made the transfer, the child had completed four reading texts. Under the individual method her enthusiasm increased and she read, in addition to several library books, twenty-five textbooks from January until the end of May. In the same room was a boy who had never been able to read satisfactorily and who, as a result, greatly disliked this activity. The teacher helped him select primer and first grade level books fitted to his ability and interest, worked to build his confidence, and instructed him in methods of word attack, including phonic helps. The boy's emotional tensions quickly decreased, and his attitude and enthusiasm improved when he realized that the eyes of the group were on their own work and not on him and his deficiencies. His progress, in terms of increase in grade level of reading, was not great that year, but he had acquired success sufficient to develop an interested, wholesome attitude towards reading which promised effective learning in the future.

The writer would like to recommend that teachers consider individualized reading carefully and with open minds. It is a method that should be developed gradually, in the light of the teacher's understanding and abilities and of its place in the satisfaction of pupil needs. Some prefer to initiate the plan in the highest reading groups and, as opportunity offers, to adapt it to the lower groups. Some feel that the slowest pupils will profit most from group work, but many have been highly successful in using the individual method for every student. The plan is sufficiently flexible to allow such variations as may seem desirable, but in no case should the teacher adopt the method until she has the technique well in mind and the materials available. Those who feel that the plan has great value, but who hesitate at what appear to be unreasonable demands on their time should be reassured by the testimony of those who have tried it. Once the plan has functioned long enough for the children to grasp the concept of the new method and for the teacher to feel secure in its handling, the work of the teacher is no greater than under the group method, while the rewards, both to pupil and teacher, are immeasurably greater.

# HOW ONE SCHOOL READ THE NEEDS OF THE SLOW READER

*Grace Garretson,*
*Teacher, Elementary School,*
*Whittier, California*

*Mrs. Garretson provides here a clear and concise description of what happens in classrooms when reading is individualized. She particularly emphasizes the factor of self-selection and how this affects children.*

THE TOPIC GIVEN us for today indicates that we are to discuss reading in relation to the slow learner. We will look at him as we find him in the middle grades. When a child reaches this level of school activity and still can not satisfactorily make meaning from the printed page, we renew our efforts to find some clue into his total make up that will enable us to help him find out how to use his own abilities. We know that unless we help him unlock the door to reading, a large share of our present day culture will be closed to him. We know that each failure in the reading experience gives the child a cause for adding another stone in his protective wall of defense, a defense even against himself. Each year he finds it more difficult to accept what teachers are earnestly trying to give, and the door to learning closes tighter. Our search for means of help has brought out many patterns of teaching and many techniques and devices, some of which are effective. But we have continued

From *Nineteenth Yearbook,* 1954 Claremont College Reading Conference. Reprinted with the permission of the Conference.

to keep the weak reader in a group of weak readers. Does this practice perpetuate reading difficulties? If we don't maintain such a group, then how shall we help him?

The plan that is to be discussed today was used by several teachers in Whittier this last year. We call it "Self-Selection in Reading." It is not a new idea. The idea has been discussed by many educators, and many experiments have been tried. *We have worked with the idea that reading is a language* PROCESS *and not a language subject*. We have made our reading time a learning situation rather than just learning to read. We have tried to put into actual practice the belief that interest, purpose and individual help will improve the reading abilities of all learners. Our results in a very short time have exceeded our expectations.

This program was not started for the slow learner specifically. It was started because we felt it held promise for all children. However, each teacher who has used the plan has found her slow or weak readers showing the greatest improvement. At any rate their improvement has been the most noticeable. When a child is allowed to use material of his own choosing, move at his own pace, in an atmosphere where how he moves is no longer public classroom concern, he relaxes his defenses and begins to feel the security of accomplishment. With this emphasis, some children have dared to tackle reading situations far beyond their abilities and succeed in very satisfying ways. A child, for instance, who refused to work on a simple book, and the word study involved, exerted untold energies to follow a fourteen year old cowboy through an exciting experience with cattle rustlers. A child who reads something because he wants to read it, and enjoys the reading, is on the way to getting meaning from that printed page.

The program follows this pattern: A child may choose material that interests him. He may choose it because the pictures, the title, or some classmate's reference to the book, attracted him. He may choose it because he is sure he can handle it, or because it looks short and he wants the feeling of satisfaction that comes with completing a book in a short time. He does not have to tell why he chooses the material, though he usually does sooner or later. He may read at his own speed. He may have individual help and thus not be classed with any group. He reports his work. He first decides how he will use the book, if he will read it all or just part of it, and how he intends to report it. He makes a record of the book and his intent of its use. If he changes his mind on either, he discusses the change and the reasons with his teacher and satisfactory adjustments are made.

The procedure of work followed a general pattern in all rooms using the plan, but details were adjusted to fit personality differences and room limitations. Books were made available in a variety of ways. Some teachers grouped the books according to subject and had the groups in different areas of the room, each group being labeled. Other teachers preferred to have several book centers for easy access but with all subjects and all reading difficulties found in each group. In this way there was no congestion at any time in the choice of books. With this second arrangement, while browsing, a child had the opportunity of being attracted to a type of reading he had not thought of before. Whatever the arrangement the necessity is to have a wide choice of books in all areas of interest and in a wide span of reading ability.

Since a child was to be the one to determine what he would read, there was no teacher grouping on ability level. There were times when two or more children found they had chosen the same book and gathered to discuss the book, in some cases to read aloud to each other for a short time or to read aloud to each other the parts that most interested them. This led to the making of new friendships, an additional value. Occasionally a teacher used a sociogram to determine a group for some instructional work, reporting or discussing of books being read. It sometimes proved expedient for the teacher to gather around her the children having difficulty with the books they had chosen. Here she was readily available for words, or help over a rough spot even though each child was still doing his individual reading. This arrangement gave the teacher an added chance to record types of help needed in word attacks and word building. Each teacher grouped or not as she felt the need for help or encouragement. The definite point that was carried out by all was that there should be no grouping on the basis of ability.

In the selection of books each child was allowed to browse. He could select a book, read a little, return it and try another. A limit of time to make final choices of the book he was to use, was established. He was then held to using the book he had chosen. Some readers knew immediately what they wanted to read and were eager to start. This included weak as well as strong readers. Other children, unused to any kind of choosing, had a harder time. It was here that the teacher had a chance to help a child do some real thinking about himself, his interests, his capacities and his chances for growth in reading. With this chance to browse and discuss with his guide and helper, he discovered interests he didn't realize he had. To children already interested in reading this was a most exciting adventure. They were thrilled to be allowed to make individual decisions and then to read unhampered or uncontrolled. They soon finished their books and were back to repeat the process of choice. Some children showed surprising skill in reading which wasn't apparent under normal group processes. If repeated choices occurred in the same field, the teacher suggested or requested that some other field or interest be pursued. There were few cases reported where this was necessary. Most children cooperated completely on the plan of the reading program, that all interest fields were available and after they had read one or two books in one area they should turn to another.

At the beginning of the plan and from time to time it was discussed how books were to be used. Each time a child chose a book he would decide how he would use it, and he recorded the name of his book and his decision as to its use on a card in a card file box. In most cases the entire book was read. Sometimes a child preferred to read only one story from a collection of stories; or only the poems from a book containing different types of material. One child looked for animal stories. Reading was silent unless as before mentioned some children gathered to read to each other, or when a child chose a certain portion to read to the group or entire class when making a report of the book. When a particular story appealed as a good story for oral reading, the child requested that he be allowed to use that story on audience reading day. One interesting use of books in a group situation occurred when three boys who were very good friends, but were reading at very different levels, gathered to discuss their books. Each boy had chosen a book on his level of reading ability but all books were about horses. They shared their findings and incidentally they helped the slowest reader with many words.

A teacher's opportunity for individual help is enhanced. She learns to know the child in a friendly way not possible in a reading group. She becomes a guide and interested friend, not a teacher testing for information. The child becomes more relaxed in his reaction to teacher's help for together they can discuss difficulties of some books, the way stories develop, or the ways books are written. She can check comprehension, observe type of book chosen and thus guide growth in tastes. A teacher can also learn more fully than any test results can give her, how much is really being accomplished. For children needing definite vocabulary building, the back side of the child's card is a place for such a record that will direct her in her planning. Children were eager to read to their teacher a particular happening, a passage that to them was an interesting way of describing something, or a part that especially attracted their interest. Each child seemed eager to report on the books he liked. Many readers recorded new or interesting words they found. The times when the teacher gathered a group around her for ready help were valuable for individual help and a chance for her to be sure of the progress being made.

The book reports followed many different patterns. A section or short story prepared for audience reading, a dramatization of a short story that three or four children had read and wished to report together; a drawing which was explained to the class; or a short oral review, are a few of the ways that were used for reporting. Some science experiments were performed to show the class something learned on the reading hour. Some books seem to lend themselves best to written reviews. Oral reviews and written reviews were specially good forms to use quite often as they form the natural tie with all the language arts. To make written reviews the child asked for or looked up words he needed. In his oral reviews he used the new expressions and new words he had discovered. Each child kept a record of the ways in which he reported each book. In this way he could see if he was using variations in his reporting program. Several children in the different rooms tried to see how many different ways they could use to report their reading. One teacher asked each child to use a card for each book read. On it they recorded the name of the book, the author, and wrote a short paragraph giving their reactions to the book, or a statement about the book, whatever he, the reader, felt would help some one else in his decision about reading that book. Several cards, of course, appeared for the popular books, some in favor and some not so favorable. This teacher reported that the cards were repeatedly read by other children who were ready to choose new materials.

The outcomes of our short experiment have been many and extremely gratifying. With all of us the first noticeable outcome was an increased desire to read on the part of each child, regardless of reading ability. There was a lengthening of the attention span in reading. This in itself demonstrated that purpose and personal interest lead to new accomplishments. There was a definite increase in word mastery by the slow learners. Increased self respect was very evident. The child who was allowed to perform at his own level of ability without any comparison, found school work more interesting. He was no longer considered at the foot of the class. In his program the teacher expected no more than a child was capable of giving, which again removed a tension. The child who once felt isolated in reading began to discuss books with his friends and sometimes read with them. Self-esteem rose and he was off to new efforts. One very weak reader wanted to report to the entire class a book he had read and enjoyed. Considering his ability and his previous antagonisms, this was a real accomplishment. He gave the name of the book, the author and illustrator, showed two illustrations and related one exciting event. He also spoke of the length of the book and then finished with this remark, "It's a book anyone in this class can read, I'm sure, and I recommend it to you because it's very interesting." His eagerness to find another book was testimony to the increased self-esteem he had gained by completing and having the opportunity of recommending a book to the class. In addition to this, the type of book he chose indicated he was increasing in his understanding of words and phrases. As each child repeatedly was allowed to choose and his choice for himself was accepted, as he found he could determine his method of reporting, he sensed the fact that he was being trusted. It was expected of him that he would learn at his own speed and that expectation, without any dictation, gave him an inner confidence and a determination to meet trust.

This program gave each child the chance to develop in a wider way. As he formed a purpose of his own for his reading and then carried out his plan, he realized the good and the bad in his own procedures. In helping the weak reader to select books he could handle, even though he needed much help, then giving him the help and encouragement to complete the task, the teacher helped him also to progress toward the independence he needed. A child who has difficulty often objects to the book you choose for study as a "baby book, too easy," even though the words are beyond his knowledge. But left to his own choice he may do as did one of my boys. When George had made sure I really meant he could read whatever he chose, absolutely anything in the room he wanted, he flew for the book he had previously objected to working on because he felt it was too easy. "Now," he said, "I'll read this today—I know I can finish it this afternoon."

Without exception more reading was done by each individual child than had been done before—even on the part of the exceptionally weak reader, and there was much more pleasure afforded all readers. Desire to read was increased because the material was to their own liking and of their own choosing. They became more discriminating about the books. They were anxious to share something new so they seemed to feel that each time they should share their accomplishments in a new way.

All of us who worked felt that the alert child who had capacities and desired to advance could and did grow without feeling retarded, and also that the child who previously had worked to try to keep up, relaxed and was more comfortable in his work. Sometimes the child is capable, but when contrasting himself with others in his old reading group, feels they are so much better than he that he develops feelings of inferiority that inhibit his real ability.

As children were given opportunity to explore and read about things that interested them, they also discovered there were many things to read about and interests grew. A report of a book enjoyed by one reader stimulated others to want to read the same book. This occurred several times when the child, while browsing, was sure he didn't want to read the book which he later found very engaging.

We felt that this type of teaching would carry over into life situations. When a child dislikes his reading experiences at school he is certainly less likely to seek reading for leisure time activity. But a child who has been happy in his reading, has learned to choose satisfactorily from many books and has discovered he enjoys certain kinds of reading, is going to wish to continue the pleasurable experience. We had many children ask about library cards, or the possibility of borrowing school books for summer reading.

We all found that discipline relaxed. Interested children are happy and busy. The reading hour was quiet because there was no reading group working orally; there was no changing of groups with the attendant interruption of attention.

Some of the teacher's opportunities with individuals have been mentioned along the way. This aspect of the plan seemed tremendous to me. When you discuss a common interest with a child and he finds you have honestly enjoyed the same book, you erase school room tensions and forge a friendship that becomes invaluable. You let him brief the plot for you, you listen to him present his personal opinion, you discuss the humor, the exaggerations, the clear word pictures or the convincing way a book is written. The book is the interest, not any probing or testing and the child is relaxed and interested. There is opportunity for you to lead a child into judgments and evaluations as you discuss characters or incidents of the book. Children enjoy comparing stories and books by the same author or books of similar topics written by different authors. As for the struggling reader, you have no misunderstanding of his needs with this personal approach. You realize his strengths and weaknesses and can much more quickly discover the techniques that will help him develop his own abilities. As you discuss his story, you make note of the areas in which you will help him later in his reading problems. You can help him clarify sequences or important details, and have him read aloud to you some section. You can help him attain the attitude that what he thinks about a book is important. His comparisons and evaluations will have a bearing on his future reading. When he reviews a book to a group or to the entire class he may interest some one else in that book. What a boost to personal satisfaction that experience is to one who has been slow!

I have reported the work done by 4th, 5th and 6th grade teachers who have used the program. It was also used on the 2nd grade level with very significant results. Selection and reading were individual. The teacher worked always with groups around her for ready help. These groups were friendship groups and varied through the year. Each child read some of his book to the teacher, she visited with him about his book and kept all of her records on individual cards for each child. Reports were given at circle time when all were ready to listen.

Getting meaning from the symbols on the printed page is only a part of the total reading. But it is the part with which teachers wrestle year after year. Teaching reading is again only part of our daily task. The heart of all teaching is to help each child in his life problems of fitting into the society in which he finds himself. Self selection reading opens vistas to a teacher in child understanding that are limited only by her own vision. The social implications are numerous. Through it all, the total class plans together on certain problems, small groups work together at times with never the same exact membership and sometimes it is teacher and child alone. As the weak reader develops inner confidence, receives help where he needs help and encouragement devoid of any ridicule, all the walls of self defense seem to crumble and he settles into his own stride and accomplishments.

It is impossible to mention all the ramifications. To do so would be to report the contacts with each child. This is an individualized program and while it increases work for the teacher, the visible progress and interest of each child is exceedingly heart-warming. A teacher needs more than ever to study each child—his background, his peer group relationships, his attitudes about himself, in fact, his whole problem. This program gives here a better chance at that study since she works with him alone. It may be that fear is holding him back and she needs to help him find something he can do well and strengthen his courage. It seems perfectly clear that curtailment of reading is tied up with many personality factors; pressure from home, too difficult books, competition with peers and the resultant inferiority feelings of constant failure. In personal contact teaching, the teacher learns many things that give her the clues for helping. It is a different approach. We know that we need to combine some of the old routines with the new. Undoubtedly we need to follow our clues to individual word needs with the proper developmental help. But our experiment has proved to those of us who have used it, that comfortable working conditions, adequate individual help and the realization that each child has a rhythm of his own in learning, are more important tools than formal techniques.

# INDIVIDUALIZING READING EXPERIENCE

*Mabel L. Johnson,*
*Teacher,*
*Long Island City, New York*

*Mrs. Johnson describes in this article how she pro-*
*ceeded with her fifth grade class. She includes some*
*quotations from children's records and gives hints to*
*teachers about keeping records. Her class had thirty-*
*six pupils with reading scores ranging from 3.1 to 8.6*
*and with IQ's from 90 to 148.*

LAST YEAR I became quite dissatisfied with my reading program. Using the standard scores and my own judgment as a basis for grouping I used three basic readers with accompanying workbooks and exercises. Suitable provisions were made for the fast readers and for the few top scorers. But I felt this reading was becoming stereotyped, deadening, and fruitless considering my preparation time. I felt I was erecting a barrier by continuing this "assignment" of a story, discussing it, then rehashing the story again through the provided exercises, varied as they were.

After a New York University reading conference, I decided to use a really individualized and natural group formation type of reading. We had some provisions in our school and classroom for extended reading during free time, but I decided to

From *New York State Education,* June, 1951. Reprinted with the permission from *New York State Education.*

conduct that kind only with organization and thoughtful planning.

## The Background of the Group

My class was a fifth year group of thirty-six active children. Their IQ's ranged from 90 to 148, with the class median 114. According to the standardized reading tests, they entered the fifth grade with scores from 3.1 to 8.6 and a median of 5.5. The class showed as much variance in personalities as in general abilities. They had a genuine interest in books, loved to read, and had had many planned experiences with books. Only a few children owned good books but all eagerly sought any added new books.

## We Begin Together

First I discussed this new venture with our principal. He gave his permission as well as his whole-hearted and active cooperation. Then I explained to the class that we were planning something different in reading, that each child should make his choice of a book to read in the reading time in place of the three basic readers. What surprise and joy!

I gathered the new books recently purchased, some sample copies, and a few books from the children's personal libraries. I supplemented these with twenty books borrowed from the public library for a four-week period. We started with sixty-six different books and we never had fewer to choose from. Each four weeks I acquired another group from the public library, more sample copies, and groups of ten books borrowed from the library by children. Books were of all types, from Lamb's *Tales of Shakespeare* to simple fairy tales. Our collection included animal stories, biographies, poetry books, technical and scientific stories, and many others. Almost every child's taste was adequately satisfied.

## The Reading Lesson Itself

First I briefly introduced each of the sixty-six books and in a special period each child chose his first book. What eager enthusiasm and long request lists!

At the start of the first lesson each child had the book he had chosen. We set up a conference reading center of two chairs for one child and myself. Daily I listed the names of ten children that I planned to confer with. For some it was merely a minute to share a book with me, to ask a question, or to answer my questions. Daily I endeavored to meet with the four children who still needed much help in reading techniques. Sometimes the time did not allow all ten conferences.

During this time the rest of the class read and changed their books. The books were located close to the conference center so that I could advise or guide if and when necessary. There were no discipline problems. What a pleasure it was to see a child lean over and quietly but enthusiastically tell his neighbor about a book he was reading! It might be some funny part, something exciting, or something unusual he had to share. But all really read.

About five minutes before the end of the allotted time, I always gave a warning signal to stop at some suitable place. Occasionally a child would plead for time to find out the fate of a beloved hero.

During the last five minutes, about five children acted as book salesmen telling something interesting that would "sell" their books to the class. Usually request lists lengthened after these talks.

At times the sharing of books provided natural formation of groups. Children who had read the same books got together for discussion, for planning a reproduction, or for planning a play about one part of the story. Children who liked the same story sometimes read together. Two or three children at times gathered in a far corner to read poetry aloud. This tendency to form small groups temporary in their make-up was based on real interests or needs. Sometimes I met with one of these little groups.

## We Kept Records

Records had to be different in this individualized reading program. We decided to keep a small notebook in diary fashion. No limits were set on the amount to be written daily but each child was required to indicate how he had spent his allotted reading time of about forty minutes. His pages might be like these:

### April 5

Today I chose a book called *Misty of Chincoteague*.[1] I read from pages 1 to 45. I am sure I will like it because horse stories are my favorites. I'm going to take it home tonight.

### April 8

I think *His Dog* that I started today is just about right for my reading ability. I found out that collies do not like to swim. I also had a conference with Miss Johnson.

In that same notebook new words and meanings were recorded. Truthfully we had more voluntary dictionary seeking than ever before. At times we played a crossword puzzle game using these new words.

Besides that personal diary, I kept a four by six card for each child. Upon completion of a book or stories in a book, a child would fill in the name of the book, date, and comment. Of course, I had no definite way of knowing the authenticity of these records. Neither did I have any sure way of knowing whether the assigned stories were read. The intense interest and

[1] Marguerite Henry, Rand McNally.

intelligent discussions of books were my proofs in this method.

In my plans I listed all the books we were using. Here, too, I kept the children's names and indicated dates of conferences and sales talks. Individual difficulties needing remedial attention were also noted here.

## What Did We Gain?

The children were absolutely delighted with this way of reading. They talked about it and wrote about it in many personal letters. Parents spoke about the enthusiasm at home, and many new and good books were added to personal libraries. The quiet way in which books were shared during reading time, the kindly way of helping one another with new words, and the excellent recommendations of books reflected fine new attitudes and interests.

When our principal asked about reading in our classroom, the beaming faces, the satisfied expressions, backed up by valid reasons for the enthusiasm, were ample proof for him, too, of its value.

In the three-month period the greatest number of books read by any child was thirty-six and the least was six books. (The child who read only six books would probably have just about finished one basic reader and very little extra reading on his own initiative.)

We didn't neglect our oral story reading, or our needed reading techniques. Outlining, skimming, and key words were all taken care of in our social studies work where they were needed.

Our reading scores at the end of the fifth year ranged from 4.4 to 9.4, with the class median of 7.2. While I realize there are too many factors to compare our beginning scores with these scores accurately, still I believe that the class showed definite growth.

# WHEN I FIRST STARTED TEACHING

Tape Recorded Comments

of One Teacher

*June McLeod,*
*Helping Teacher, Levittown Public Schools,*
*Long Island, New York*

> *As the researcher in an evaluation study of the*
> *master's level, preservice teacher education program*
> *at New York University, Miss McLeod recorded an*
> *interview with a teacher who tried to teach reading*
> *by means of ability grouping and basal texts but could*
> *not make it work.*

BEGINNING TEACHERS, and possibly some not-so-beginning, are likely to think that there must be *a way,* a *one* way, to teach reading to children. So certain are some students in pre-service education that such a method exists that frequently, I'm sure, they feel that their college teachers are deliberately keeping that way hidden from them. That a number of approaches to the teaching of reading, equally in harmony with the general philosophy of child development may be used effectively seems hard to accept. Hence it is refreshing to find a beginning teacher who has caught the basic ingredients needed for optimum growth in children to such an extent that she reflects a fine educational philosophy and can also withstand pressures pulling her in an opposite direction.

From *Reading Teacher,* April, 1954. Reprinted by permission of the author and the International Reading Association.

Such a teacher is the one who is quoted in this article. She had learned that children are individuals, each unique in his development, growing at different rates. In her first job she attempted to apply these principles to a reading program. She refused to use the customary slow, middle, and fast ability groupings. Instead she organized her reading program on an individualized basis.

However, her inexperience prevented her from operating in a smooth fashion, and she became confused by the multiplicity of mechanical problems that arose by having children in different places at different times in different books. This confusion led her to admire the seemingly serene classrooms of the neighboring teachers. They used homogeneous groupings of "Bluebirds," "Robins" and "Canaries," with every child within a group reading the same page in the same book. After five months this teacher moved to another school. This gave her the opportunity she thought she wanted—to get a new start in a reading program and to use the seemingly serene methods of her peer teachers in the first situation.

## Her Own Story

Here is the story of what happened. It is told in her own words, as she told it in an interview with the writer. The words hold such quality of respect for the basic individuality of respect for the basic individuality of children with a disturbing confusion of philosophy that they seem to be worthy of verbatim quote as they came from the tape recording:

"When I first started teaching, I went all out for meeting the needs of individual children, especially in reading. When I came in and found other teachers had them in set groups, I tried to start that way so that I'd have something to begin with. But later on I couldn't see how it would work when children are so different. So in the first grade, after a month, all the children were in a different place and I even had a different page for each child so if a child didn't remember I'd know. Sometimes I heard each child read alone every day. Not every child every day, but I'd call up one group like *Rain and Shine*. They were in different places. I'd ask the child, 'Did you read this story? What is the first sentence?' And so on. I'd go around and help them.

"But it got *so complicated* that when I changed to this new school, I decided I was going to keep them in their books and all in the same place because I got lost the last time. I felt they had enough supplementary books and library books. So I had plenty of materials, and there was no reason they couldn't be guided in their books for part of the time. *So* I was going to introduce *new words,* introduce *the story every day* and talk about it. But *again* it happened!

"The children were just reading off on their own. Some were just so fast and such good readers that they would come up and say, 'I read it already,' even if I still had the books on the shelf and hadn't taken them down. I felt like a fool. It was just so ridiculous to go through that formality. They'd already read it, and it wasn't interesting to them. And so *again* they branched out, and I never was able to keep them all together at one place, like finish a story today, finish a story tomorrow. And so I began to do the same thing I did in the first grade, and they all went on their own. I had them up, I had them read individually and I have right now one group, *Friends and Neighbors,* who stay together because they seem so fit for it. They read one story a day and it works out. And one other group, *More Friends and Neighbors*. The rest of them just go out on their own in different books.

"Even the slow readers can't keep together. I used to keep them together and I *knew* they weren't getting it, even silently. It was just too much, too slow. They were missing words; and when someone read orally, they weren't interested. Their minds would wander, and so I had to take them up alone. And they feel better too; they don't feel like they're labeled in a group . . . And I think that it worked."

## Highlights of Her Experience

What can be highlighted from this teacher's experience as she related it? First, when she began teaching she had a definite guiding principle in mind: "Meet the needs of individual children." Second, she was aware of the other teachers and it was important to her to gain acceptance and recognition from them. In this instance there was a conflict between what she believed about children and her need to be accepted. She chose first to seek acceptance by not being too different from the others. But with her belief in meeting the needs of individual children and her sensitivity to these needs, set groups did not work out. Therefore she developed a reading program that was in keeping with her orientation toward children. But she was unsure.

Two factors made her unsure of her individualized approach. One was, in her own words, "It got so complicated." The other was the lack of support, though not necessarily criticism, from both fellow teachers and those in supervisory capacity. So in a new situation she determined to try set groupings a second time. But *"again* it happened!" Those seven-year-olds, like the younger sixes, could not be molded and shaped to theoretical averages and grade norms. At one end of the scale, they were "just reading off." At the other end, "Even the slow readers can't keep together." Predetermined, fixed groupings—perhaps better than no groupings—still did not really provide an opportunity for each child to function at his optimum level. But by now the conflict between meeting children's needs and her own need for acceptance was shrinking. No doubt this was partly because a little experience had given her some security and mechanical know-how. In another part of the interview she also indicated that she was getting support from the administration and acceptance by her peers even though she was approaching reading in a slightly different manner.

She is still not altogether sure, but in the repeat performance some of the original problems seem to have disappeared. No longer is the process described in terms of "complicated." A positive attitude is noted: "They feel better, too," and "I think it worked."

Here is not the working out of someone else's method, but rather a way that seems to work for one person because it is intrinsically her own, developed from her own insights into and understanding of children's needs. It works because she and her group seem "so fit for it."

I'm sure many young persons with this same fine sensitivity for children and with real potential for teaching are entering the teaching profession each year. Will they succumb to the mediocrity, patterned, unimaginative, uncreative, same-as-everybody-else way of handling reading—it may or it may not be "teaching"—because of fear or criticism of the teacher in the next room or the supervisor or principal? I hope not, but it's not an easy pressure to withstand. Given an accepting, friendly, supportive, encouraging, free-to-experiment environment, beginning teachers might discover many doors opening upon new and never-thought-of worlds. The big question is: will we give them a chance?

# AN INDIVIDUALIZED
# READING PROGRAM

*Bessie Maxey,*
*Teacher,*
*Public Schools, Villa Grove, Illinois*

*Mrs. Maxey describes how she was able to individualize her first grade reading program. The article is notable for its practicality. It contains suggestions for independent work and describes a unique pattern of pairing of children for reading conferences.*

EACH CHILD has his own individual pattern for mental, physical, and emotional development. He may grow in each of these at the same rate of speed or may develop faster or slower in one particular phase.

No one is greatly concerned if Susie walks a few months earlier or later than her cousin or neighbor. It is not considered of terrific concern if Jimmy hasn't talked as soon as his playmate.

Yet as soon as a child approaches the age of six and starts to school the individual growth pattern is set aside. All are expected to master the art of reading at an equal rate of speed. A child who doesn't soon feels inferior and disgraced. These feelings form blockages that hinder and harm his future growth in the mastery of reading. A keen dislike for reading may even be developed.

Much has been written and taught concerning individual differences, the desirability of meeting individual needs, and letting each child develop at his own rate of speed. Yet the gap between theory and practice has often been very wide. Too many teachers have been confronted with large enrollment in their classes and have said, "That all sounds fine, but it can't be done when you have so many in your room."

In a room of thirty or more, the primary teacher usually divides the children into two or three reading groups—rapid learners, average, and slower readers. In some cases, each group is given a different type of help with the intention of meeting individual differences, yet all are expected to read the same material each day. Some teachers do a little better by letting the groups advance at different speeds through the prescribed material, yet they expect even the slower-moving ones to complete it before the year is over.

The usual procedure is to have each group of children read together for fifteen or twenty minutes. This permits each child actually to read only a page or portion of a page. The rest of the time he is supposedly watching and reading silently along with the child who is reading aloud, but more often he is planning what he will do when school is out or may even be looking at something else. In order for each child to read a part of the day's story, it is repeated several times. The child who learns readily is subjected to unnecessary repetition and becomes bored. The slower-learning child leaves the group mentally and fails to learn even as much as he is capable of learning.

Because we felt the ineffectiveness of such methods, the teachers in our school have set up the specific goal of meeting each child's individual needs and growth patterns. Every child is permitted to learn to read at his own rate. He is kept with his own age group but reads at his own reading level.

The last two years, I have added a few features with my first-year pupils. My room environment is set up to permit an activity program. There are puzzles to work, a playhouse nook, plenty of painting materials and space to paint, free-hand cutting materials, clay, crayons, farm toys, dollhouse, jumbo blocks, game board, science corner, workbench with materials and tools, paste, balls, and books. The first period of the day we call our sharing time and the children share experiences, ask questions, and show things they have brought to school. Many of these lead us into interesting units of work full of enriching experiences.

Following this period each child is given some work for which he is individually responsible. When this work is completed he may choose any of the things provided for him to use. There are two rules. Each child must be busy at something, and he must do it quietly enough so those reading are not disturbed. Most of the creative work related to our units is done by committees or individuals at this time. Problems needing the teacher's help are saved and brought up between reading groups or after all have had a reading turn.

When children are working or playing together they show their real selves. It is while they are thus engaged that a teacher gets an insight into their personalities and emotional needs so that she knows how to help them become better citizens.

The children are divided into partner groups for reading. These partners are as nearly equal in reading interests and abilities as possible. The two who read together take turns at being listener and teacher. They leave their activity to read and then resume it when their turn is over.

Although my main attention is with the two who are reading, I am able to watch the others. The children who are not reading are free to come to me for approval of work done; or they wait for help between reading groups.

I find this type of program makes for happier children and

thus for better schoolroom citizens. Each child is given the help he himself needs and he advances in reading ability at his own rate of learning.

The first year I had this type of program, my enrollment was thirty-seven. This year it is twenty-seven. It is a great advantage to have the smaller enrollment but the program will work with the larger.

So, teachers, let's not hide behind the old alibi, "It's fine in theory but won't work in my situation." Give it a try. It has given me new impetus, a new challenge, a new feeling of joy in actually living with my pupils and happiness in watching them grow and develop into the best each can be.

| Chapter | YOU NEED GOOD LIBRARIES |
|---|---|

# Chapter

# 8.

## YOU NEED GOOD LIBRARIES
## TO TEACH READING TODAY

*Nancy Larrick,*
*Education Director, Children's Books, Random*
*House*

*Dr. Larrick, through her extensive experience as
teacher, author, and editor, has long been interested
in the optimum use of trade books in a school setting.
In this article she discusses the relationship of such
books in the library to the instructional reading program in the classroom. Her description of individualized practices is clear and helpful.*

A NEW LIBRARY-CENTERED plan for teaching
reading is being advocated by many leaders in the field of education who report dramatically successful results in terms of
children's progress and their interest in reading. Briefly stated,
this new teaching technique is a plan whereby each child selects
the book he wants to read and then proceeds at his own pace
with his teacher helping him individually.

For the child this procedure means reading the things he is
interested in without being pushed or held back by other children, and it means getting the help he needs when he needs it.

For the teacher it means increased pupil interest, greater
freedom to work with individual children, and the satisfaction
of seeing more children reading better.

For the librarian it means a new crop of library patrons who

From *Junior Libraries,* September 15, 1954. Used by permission.

are brought up using the library and making the most of its treasure stores.

What is this new trend? Educators refer to this new trend as *individualized reading* because the emphasis is on the needs of each child and the help which can be given to him individually. Many who have tried this plan for teaching reading insist that it is not difficult even with a large class and that the dividends paid off in increased pupil enthusiasm more than repay the first upheaval and adjustment to a new plan of teaching.

Instead of meeting with a small group of ten or twelve pupils, the teacher meets with one child at a time, hearing him read for a couple of minutes, helping him with his special problems, and making a record of his progress. If she finds that three or four need the same kind of help, she will gather them together in one corner for a few minutes of special coaching. But such groups are completely flexible, with constantly changing personnel and purposes. While the teacher is helping one or two children, the others are reading silently or working on related activities.

When contrasted with the usual plan of three or four reading groups per class, this plan has many distinct advantages:

Each child selects the books he will read; therefore he feels greater interest in what he is reading and makes a greater effort to succeed.

Each child reads at his own pace; therefore he is not held up by and does not hold up others who might have been assigned to his reading group under previous arrangements.

Each child is taught the reading skills when he needs them; thus he sees these skills as important and worth achieving.

Because the individualized reading program is based on children's free choice of reading materials, it has occasionally been confused with what is sometimes called "free reading" or "recreational reading." A child may use the same library books for both kinds of reading and may put the same enthusiastic drive into both. But to the teacher there is a great distinction—individualized reading to her means a time for instruction and development of skills, while recreational reading means reading for fun and relaxation with little or no instruction from the teacher.

Without a goodly array of library books the individualized reading plan cannot work. Its success depends upon the psychological advantage of letting children choose what they want to read and letting them find the books they feel are within their reach. The word-of-mouth recommendation from one child may be enough to send several others after the same book as their next selection. This kind of momentum could never have operated in the old scheme of things where every child was reading from the same page of the same reader, whether or not he found the content interesting.

Only those who have worked with children can appreciate the terrific drive that grows out of a child's curiosity or interest. A new radio station in one small town brought a deluge of questions from the fifth graders. What was the tower for? Why were local programs clearer than those originating out of town? What connection did the local station have with network programs? Capitalizing on such questions the teacher and librarian helped children find books and pamphlets about radio and television so that they could read further and bring in their findings.

In another school, *Life's* science feature on dinosaurs appealed to one third-grader so much that he brought a copy to school, along with all the excitement and curiosity that a nine-year-old can generate. This was what he wanted to read— and no one could stop him! With that driving determination, he soon had many others fired with the same subject. The result was that a group of eight boys read everything they could locate on dinosaurs and the strange beasts of the past. Some of them pushed their reading skills to cope with books on a fourth and fifth grade level. For them reading was fun because it had a purpose that grew out of their own driving interest.

In both of these situations the teacher and librarian made the most of children's interests. They encouraged them to read books about the subject that was hottest at that moment instead of prodding them to read the next story in a textbook which did not stir their interest or answer their most urgent questions.

A number of studies have been made of children's interests. One of the most significant findings is that children's interests change as our society changes. Therefore some of the things that were of great interest to ten-year-olds in 1940 might not be so important to ten-year-olds in 1954—and television program that was never listed in a 1940 study would probably rate a top place among children's choices today. Furthermore, the choices and attitudes of city children are known to be quite different from those in a small rural community. Thus, it seems apparent that we cannot accept research findings about children's interests without asking how recently the study was made and in what kind of community.

All of this points to the importance of teacher-librarian co-operation in determining what children are most interested in. Frequently teachers have asked their pupils to fill in a brief check list or questionnaire about their hobbies, activities, most urgent questions, favorite stories, favorite radio and TV programs. And in many cases the alert librarian can pick up some further hint that will help the teacher find a special interest on which to build a reading project for some particular child.

Yet the interests of the child are only one determining factor in his search for the right book. He wants it to be an interesting subject, but he also wants it on his reading level. In an uncanny way he will reject one book after another in his search for "the right book." He has no measuring rod to determine the reading level of the book, but he knows when it is right for him and is much happier when he has had a hand in determining whether the book fits him.

Just what range of reading levels can the teacher and librarian expect to be in each classroom group? The most authoritative answer to this question seems to be that given by Willard C. Olson of the University of Michigan in *The Packet,* service bulletin of D. C. Heath and Company.

Thus, according to Dr. Olson, a typical group of fifth graders will be reading on nine different "book levels"—Grade 1 through Grade 9. Children in such a classroom will need books on as many levels if they are to be read easily and comfortably and if they are to progress naturally. Certainly it would be a farce to expect all such children to read from one reader or even to read from books on the three levels selected for slow, average, and fast groups.

The new individualized reading program is a library-centered program. It presupposes a wide variety of books in some accessible place where children can browse and make their own selections. How well they choose their books will depend in part on the way the books are introduced and displayed. If the librarian has been able to introduce certain books to one class through storytelling, reading aloud, or capsule summary, she has alerted those youngsters to the possibility of those particular books. If she has displayed the jackets or perhaps children's evaluations of the books, she may be able to reach still more youngsters. If she has given teachers an opportunity to explore new books, she may be able to enlist their support in advertising her wares. And because they know something of the books in advance, children will be able to make their selections more easily and more effectively.

With such a program, learning to read becomes a great adventure whereby children explore the world of children's books and sample the joys of reading.

Chapter

# 9.

# INDIVIDUALIZED TEACHING
# OF READING

*Jill Bonney,*
*Reading Helping Teacher, and*
*Levin B. Hanigan,*
*Elementary Supervisor and Director of Reading*
*Program,*
*Arlington County Public Schools,*
*Arlington, Virginia*

*Mrs. Bonney and Mr. Hanigan discuss and describe*
*from an administrative and supervisory viewpoint*
*individualized reading as they have seen it develop in*
*their school system. The section called "Teacher and*
*Pupil Activities" is a good description of how a class-*
*room works under such a program.*

GENERALLY, CHILDREN in a classroom are grouped for instructional purposes. This procedure usually results in a minimum of three reading groups corresponding roughly to good readers, average readers, and poor readers. But there are times when every child needs special attention. Within these groupings there are children who do not exactly "fit," as many teachers express it. They may be either a little slow for the group, but not slow enough for another group, or they may be approaching the next highest level, but not quite good enough to fit into that group. Also, children within each group have a wide range of interests.

From *National Elementary Principal,* September, 1955, *Thirty-Fourth Year-book.* Used by permission.

The individualized teaching of reading, with emphasis upon the children's individual interests and levels of development, is designed to meet these needs. It is a developmental program with specific aims and definite procedures. Reading is taught fundamentally as well as incidentally. The information that follows reflects the questions of classroom teachers who have discussed the program in staff meetings and workshops.

## Basic Philosophy

Several ideas lie behind the individualized approach to teaching reading. Together they form the basic philosophy of our program.

### Reading as an Individual Skill.

Reading is fundamentally an individual skill and, as such, can best be learned when instruction most nearly meets the individual's needs. This process does not eliminate all group procedures; instead, it increases the number of groups. It necessitates that groups be flexible, temporary, and formed for teaching a particular skill or for sharing ideas gained from reading.

### Pupil-Teacher Rapport.

The success of this program depends primarily upon pupil-teacher rapport. The child needs to understand that the teacher is eager to help him at all times. He also needs to understand that the teacher is sympathetic, interested, enthusiastic, and not unduly critical of his weaknesses. Teacher and pupil together must discover weaknesses and strive to overcome them. This quality of rapport applies not only to the mechanical processes of reading, but also to other phases of the reading program, such as the selection and evaluation of reading material, the organization of reports, study skills, and leisure-time reading.

## Teacher as a Guidance and Resource Person.

While the teacher's primary responsibilities are (a) to develop a desire in children to want to read and (b) to teach them the skills to fulfil this desire, the individualized program of instruction places the teacher more emphatically in the role of a guidance and resource person than he has been heretofore. He moves about the room listening to children read, helping them with problems in their reading, noting difficulties that will need further attention, discussing concepts and understandings, and conferring about materials.

## All Must Understand Objectives.

None of the objectives stressed in other methods of reading instruction can be sacrificed because an individualized approach is used. Rather these objectives are more strongly emphasized. The basic skills (listed in any good textbook on reading) receive as much, if not more attention in this program than in any other.

However, beyond the conventional skills phase of the reading program, the individualized approach achieves additional desirable objectives. It inspires the child to read, provides broader reading experiences, instils an appreciation of fine literature of all types, develops a spirit of self-evaluation, develops an ability to evaluate literature critically, and enables children to progress at their own reading levels more satisfactorily.

The achievement of these objectives depends to a great extent upon how well teachers, pupils, parents, administrators, and supervisors understand the objectives and how hard they strive to attain them. The program will be hampered without such a cooperative approach based on mutual understanding.

## Reading Materials.

Reading should not be confined to basic readers but should embrace all kinds of materials. Many sources will be available to children in their everyday contacts.

## Evaluation.

Evaluating the results of a reading program is part of a basic philosophy of reading. The individualized approach seems to offer greater opportunity to measure the child's progress in reading for, in the final analysis, growth in reading is an individual matter to be assessed for each child.

## Open-Mindedness.

Any philosophy must admit experiment. Thus, no one method of teaching reading is best for all pupils at all times. As teachers become more experienced in the individualized approach, they will find better ways to adapt the program to their own abilities and to the abilities of their pupils.

These principles, then, form our basic philosophy of the individualized approach to the teaching of reading. They are the foundation of the detailed activities described in the remainder of this article.

## Preparation for the Program

Extensive preparation and organization are required for the launching of a program. These requirements refer particularly to the classrooms, the parents, the materials of instruction, and to the supplementary personnel.

### The Classroom.

As has been suggested, the individualized approach demands that the classroom teacher establish a good working relationship with the students. The children must realize that the teacher is there to help them with their difficulties, so that they may become better readers and have a more fervent desire to read.

Having a part in planning the reading program is vital to this wholesome working relationship. Some items that the children can help plan may include agreeing on the time for reading, setting up a book display, establishing a procedure for checking books in and out, securing books from the school and public libraries, caring for the library tables or the library corner, deciding on methods of evaluating materials read, developing procedures for keeping records of materials read, and selecting student helpers who may assist other children with their reading problems.

If the children are to feel responsible for a good reading atmosphere, the teacher should guide them into asking such questions as: Why do we want to read? Is it quiet enough for good concentration? How do we know when a book is too difficult? How can we help ourselves to become better readers? Pupil participation in answering the questions will help to stimulate the program.

### The Parents.

Parents, like the children, participate more effectively in a program which they understand and approve. The teacher should explain to them his basic philosophy of teaching reading and seek their cooperation in securing suitable reading materials. In addition, the teacher should encourage parents to visit the classroom so that they may better understand what the teacher wishes to accomplish. Informed parents can be strong supporters.

*The Materials of Instruction.*

Many and varied reading materials are essential to this type of program. Immediately the question arises, "Where does one get enough materials?" Procurement is not nearly as difficult as it may seem. Parents usually are quite willing to contribute reading material, if they know what is desired. Many public libraries will allow a teacher to sign out from 25 to 30 books at a time under his own name, and the children can obtain books on their own library cards. Also, well-stocked school libraries are important.

Resource materials, such as encyclopedias, science books, and social studies books, help children to understand that they read for many purposes other than pleasure or entertainment. In the lower grades, stories about the children and their daily experiences may be reproduced on charts and used for reading purposes. These charts may be tacked on the walls, made into class books, kept on an easel, or preserved by some other method for ready reference.

The children themselves may produce exciting reading materials. Their stories and reports may be bound with cardboard, decorated appropriately, illustrated attractively, and placed in the room library.

The children may work to more advanced levels as authors. They may become proofreaders and produce stories that are relatively free of grammatical errors and high in interest level. This type of material often has a much greater appeal because the experiences are personal ones told in words that most children comprehend readily. Sometimes these books may be put into the school library for other children in the school to read.

*The Supplementary Personnel.*

The librarian of the school plays a very important part in this type of reading program. Through frequent conferences with the classroom teacher, he soon becomes aware of the types and levels of books that are desired by a particular child. The librarian will often point out to the child a book or magazine article in which he thinks the child may be interested. The cooperation of the librarian also helps to provide a room library that may be changed from time to time. These books are attractively displayed to arouse interest.

Story telling may be another contribution of the librarian. Assisting in this activity from time to time may be parents, community members, public librarians, other children from the school, the principal, or other school personnel.

At times, authors of children's books may stimulate reading through their correspondence or personal visits to the school.

## Teacher and Pupil Activities

After the classroom teacher has secured materials on all levels, he displays them in a convenient and attractive manner. Then he sets up a plan of organization with the children which will permit each one to choose the material that he wishes to read. As the children read, the teacher is free to help them with words that they may not know. Usually, extended instruction should not be given at this time in order not to interrupt their thread of thought. However there are times when immediate attention will gain greater results, depending upon the child and the type of instruction needed at the time.

The teacher may sit with different children and listen to them read aloud the portion of the story that they have been reading silently. At this time, the teacher will note children having similar difficulties in word analysis, word meaning, the understanding of ideas, oral expression of ideas, or other skills generally emphasized in any reading program. The teacher need not listen to every child read every day in order to know who needs help.

At a satisfactory time, the teacher may want to call together a few pupils who are having difficulties. It is in these small groups—always flexible, as some pupils may need very little help and others a great deal—that the greatest amount of time is spent in teaching the basic skills. At times, individuals are helped in the same way.

As the program progresses, children learn that the teacher is willing and anxious to help each child with his individual difficulties. Each child receives this help without criticism or stigma, and he responds to the teaching. Throughout this process, reading for meaning, rather than reading to pass tests, is emphasized.

The total reading period is approximately 50 minutes long. Part of this time is spent in checking and extending comprehension. There are many interesting ways to do this other than just having a child read aloud or answer questions asked by the teacher. One of the most frequently used methods is having the child simply tell his story to the entire group or to a small group who may be reading out of the same book or to those who have been reading about the same subject. Another way that the pupil may show that he has comprehended what he has read is by trying to "sell" his book or story to the group. Or a reader might tell his story as it appears to him in a make-believe crystal ball—similar to the line put out by a fortune teller. Sometimes the children may desire to illustrate, dramatize, or sing what they have read. We believe that if a pupil can tell his story accurately through these several mediums, he has comprehended the material.

The classroom teacher contributes to stimulating interest in reading through recommending books, reading parts of books, poems, stories, and other interesting materials, telling stories, arranging attractive book displays, and other similar activities. From all of this encouragement, pupils develop a wider and more intense interest in children's literature.

## Evaluation

The most commonly used types of evaluation are teacher and parent observation of children (particularly in regard to the kind of material selected, the amount of material, the difficulty of the material, the amount and kind of help needed to read successfully, and the reaction of children toward the material read, oral reading, creative writing, discussions of material read, standardized tests, teacher tests, informal inventory using basal readers, and the observed desire of children to want to read.

The reaction of children themselves are necessary to complete an evaluation. A few typical statements of pupils follow:

> I like our reading period because I can read more and better stories. I don't like it because I get so interested sometimes that I read when I shouldn't.
>
> Reading is more of a pleasure to me. I get books I really enjoy reading. It was never interesting listening to others read and missing lots of words.
>
> Since I get more help from the teacher, I work harder myself.

## Try the Individualized Approach

We believe that the individualized approach to teaching reading merits consideration by other elementary-school faculties. First they may wish to experiment with it and then they will know whether or not to extend it throughout the school.

# WHY NOT TRY SELF-SELECTION?

Mildred E. Thompson,
Reading Consultant, El Monte School District,
El Monte, California

*This article discusses the experiences of a number of teachers with their reading program; how they got started, how they kept records, what children thought about it, what teachers thought about it. Steps taken by the reading consultant to improve teaching are also discussed.*

"WHAT CAN I do to interest my seventh-grade class in reading?" This question coming from a classroom teacher was a familiar one to the group of coordinators and consultants at the grade-level meeting. "Why not try self-selection?" said one of the consultants.

This suggestion was accepted by the seventh-grade teacher who was concerned about his class. His success and enthusiasm, plus encouragement from the curriculum office, have inspired others to try this plan of reading until there are now

From *Elementary English*, December, 1956. Reprinted by permission of the author and the publishers of *Elementary English*. (The author of this article wishes to express appreciation to the following El Monte teachers for supplying the anecdotal records and other materials for this article: Victor Baird, Eugene Dixon, Bob Killian, Doris Nye, Mary Sain, Naomi Sawyer, and William Stadtlander. She also wishes to express her gratitude to Marian Jenkins, Consultant in Elementary Education, County of Los Angeles Schools, and to Dr. Richard Brown, Director of Curriculum, El Monte School District, who have by their inspiration and cooperation contributed greatly to the success of this program.)

seven teachers in the El Monte School District who are using self-selection of reading materials as a reading program.

A search for background material revealed that Dr. Willard Olson in his article on "Seeking, Self-selection, and Pacing in the Use of Books by Children," referred to self-selection as a useful concept if one is to use the seeking tendencies of children to best advance their competence in skills, attitudes, and information. Delores Cooper Palmer, in her study, "To Determine the Reaction of a Fourth Grade to a Program of Self-selection of Reading Materials," defined the term self-selection in this way:

> for purposes of this study, the term self-selection was taken to mean that children have the opportunity to choose the material they read during the regular period of reading instruction. This means that books of many types, on many subjects, and of varying degrees of difficulty were made available. The range of reading difficulty extended from beginning reading books to those labeled beyond the known ability of the most competent reader in the room.[1]

Additional helpful materials, which included Grace Garrettson's report to the Claremont Reading Conference, were assembled in a kit for each teacher in the self-selection program.

Visitations to other districts were made. Discussions with members of the curriculum office and consultants from the Los Angeles County Schools Office helped the teachers who wanted to try individualizing their reading program more exactly than the "three-group" method allows.

At the close of the second year in self-selection, it was possible to make the interesting observation that there is no *one* "best way" of handling self-selection which works for all

[1] Delores Cooper Palmer, *To Determine the Reaction of a Fourth Grade to a Program of Self-selection in Reading Materials.* Unpublished master's thesis, University of Utah, 1953, p. 1.

teachers. Each must find the way that works best for him in the keeping of records, time allotment, grouping of books, methods of reporting, audience days, etc.

An eighth-grade teacher who has thirty-seven pupils, with a class reading achievement range of six years, felt that individualized reading most nearly met the needs of his class. He was interested to find that hero stories, such as *Young Ike, Daniel Boone,* and *Ulysses S. Grant* headed the list of preferred books reported on the Springfield Interest Finder, an inventory given at the beginning of the school year. Sports books and science-fiction occupied second and third places respectively. The results of the inventory were sent to the district central library. The librarian sent sixty books of the special interest type, which were on various grade levels. These books were augmented by library books checked out by the pupils during trips to the public library, district supplementary readers, and state adopted textbooks. An additional source was the recreational kit of fifty books sent to all seventh and eighth-grade classes, which was changed six times a year.

Teachers have said, "It certainly takes a lot of books and other reading materials to carry on a successful program in Individualized Reading." Such a statement is true. Not all the materials needed come from the district library. Pupils can brings from home books and magazines which can be shared by all the class.

One teacher devised an interesting card file. A large board was placed in front of the room; on it there were thirty-seven clothespins, one for each child. Each pin held a card on which was written the student's name, the name of the book, the name of the author, the number of pages in the book, a few lines telling why the student selected the book, and his plan for reporting on the book. This file served as a checkout board for all books, as well as a source of information for students, visitors, and the teacher.

This same teacher followed the plan of having each pupil read twice a week individually for periods of five minutes or longer, depending on the need and interest. A record card was kept by the teacher on each student, listing books read, comprehension, and vocabulary needs. During another period, instruction was given in the skills in which the student needed help.

What do parents think of self-selection? According to reports received from parent conferences, they are in favor of it. One parent remarked, pretending to be disgruntled, "I used to be able to stay home on Saturdays; now, I have to take my boy to the library every week to check out more books."

Most of the teachers using self-selection evaluate it by saying, "I like it because my children like it. All of my discipline problems are solved because the children are reading books on their own achievement level and ones in which they are interested, because the books are of their own choosing." One teacher asked, "How do you *stop* them from reading? Mine take out a book as soon as they come in from recess, and start reading again as soon as spelling and arithmetic assignments are completed. It has made a wonderful change in my class, but I wonder if there is such a thing as reading too much?"

Research doesn't answer this question, but most researchers agree with Helen Robinson's view that a study of the reading interests of students is one of the most important aspects of teaching reading for teachers from the primary grades through college. Dr. Robinson explains that children learn to read more rapidly if they are interested in the materials they use in reading.

G. Frederic Kuder and Blanche B. Paulson believe that interests are such a strong motivating force that it is necessary for a teacher to know what her children's interests are in order to help them in all phases of school work. Kuder and Paulson also state that teachers in remedial work have realized success when they have used the technique of discovering a retarded reader's interests, then supplying him with books and other material on *his* reading level, thus utilizing this strong motivating force—interest.

In addition to interest inventories, Helen Robinson includes case studies, personal interviews, records of books withdrawn from libraries, diary records of books, and magazines and newspapers read during a given period of time as valid techniques for investigating reading interests. Paul Witty suggests an informal interview between the teacher and pupils, usually guided by questions.

Teachers sometimes ask the question, "How do I get students away from reading a single type of book?" Robinson believes that it is necessary in this instance to lead the students to closely allied or similar types of books. Teachers must not only satisfy a student's current interests but must also be on the alert to promote additional interests. She states, "For all children, it is the responsibility of each teacher to cultivate and encourage reading interests which are appropriate for the child's level of general maturity. Interests should expand with age, and in certain areas, they should be intensified." [2]

One seventh-grade teacher started self-selection in February because her group seemed bored and restless. The reading achievement range was from fourth grade to eleventh grade. The pupils had finished the state textbook and had read a few library books. Since February, each pupil has read an average of two books per week. The restlessness has become less evident, and the boredom has vanished. An outstanding reporting

[2] Helen Robinson, "What Research Says to the Teacher of Reading, Reading Interests," *The Reading Teacher*, Feb., 1955, p. 177.

job was done by a group that dramatized "The Legend of Sleepy Hollow." The chairman wrote the parts on slips of paper and instructed the players to *really* learn them, and they did.

This teacher used a note-book, saving a separate page for each child, on which she listed difficulties, date for each book each child read, book, and the page number for each difficulty. When asked why she liked self-selection, she replied, "I like it because the children like it, although I'll have to admit some of my scientific wizards keep me hopping to keep ahead of them. Anyone know where I can find an eleventh grade chemistry book? One of my students needs it for an experiment."

An eighth-grade teacher who had a class with a reading achievement range from fifth grade to college level reported that his group was particularly interested in early pioneer stories about Daniel Boone, Davy Crockett, and other frontier heroes. The boys' second interest was in hunting and fishing stories; the girls' major interest was in love stories. All were interested in teen-age problems, and the class presented many socio-dramas using material from *Into Your Teens,* and from articles read in the Science Research Associates booklets on teen-agers. This teacher believed that an important part of the self-selection program was the sharing of materials and ideas by the students with each other and with the teacher.

He said that he was amazed by the many different types of publications read by members of the class and by the increasing ability of many students to find stories that related to a current event. He related that because of the assignment to write an essay about the Liberty Bell, for the American Legion Contest, the students read many stories on this subject. Some read four or five articles before starting to write. The teacher thought that this was quite unusual for eighth-grade students. When asked to evaluate the program he said, "I like it because

I have more time with individual students, and I believe I am taking care of individual needs more effectively."

One eighth-grade teacher reported that the children liked self-selection, but that she wanted to see more evidence of success by means of objective testing. This point was one commonly raised; however, most teachers using self-selection agreed with the fifth-grade teacher who wrote, "Our experiment has proved to those of us who have used it that comfortable working conditions, adequate individual help, and the realization that each child has a rhythm of his own in learning are more important tools than formal techniques."

A fifth-grade teacher, after six months of self-selection, felt that his pupils' reactions to this way of reading were in proportion to their reading abilities. The accelerated readers were delighted and read many books following their own special interests. The retarded readers decided to read together in a group, from an easy supplementary reader, with teacher guidance. The teacher was very much interested in this, and he thought that possibly more guidance was needed in use of time and selection of reading materials. He agreed with other teachers that "discipline" problems had disappeared when the class was using the method of self-selection.

Marian Jenkins found that there were fewer "disciplinary" problems when self-selection was used, and many troublesome children found an absorbing interest for the first time.

During an audience day in a fifth-grade teacher's room, a girl who plans to become a nurse used several books, including a health book (fifth grade vocabulary level) and a college physiology book, to prepare her report on parts of the body, She also used original charts and a plastic torso, nicknamed Homer, discussing each part as she removed it from the torso. A boy, reporting on a book about a pony express rider, had made a diorama using a cardboard carton, earth, twigs for trees, and a plastic horse and rider. He was explaining how one rider relieved the other at pony express stations when he was asked, "Couldn't the riders stop anywhere for coffee, or anything?" "Well," he answered, "they stopped at the pony express stations for coffee. I guess you could call it the first coffee break."

A sixth-grade teacher said that his group was reading an average of two or three books a week. He found that some of the students were inclined to read materials on one topic, but he had succeeded in guiding their interests in other directions. His group had particularly enjoyed using the opaque projector, flashing illustrations and stories they had made on a screen.

Another sixth-grade teacher made a sociogram of her group at the beginning of the year. The results supported her suspicion that the class contained a boy "star" with a "cluster" surrounding him, a girl "star" with her "cluster," plus several "isolates." These "stars" were frequently poor influences on their peers, as was evidenced by anti-social acts in the audio-visual room and on the playground, which were approved by the group.

The teacher introduced self-selection as a possible way to break up the "gangs." That she was successful is borne out by the results of a second sociogram made toward the close of the school year. This chart showed the entire class in groups of twos and threes. There were no "stars," no "clusters," and no "isolates." The class enjoyed individualized reading, directing their energies to the writing of original poetry, plays, and stories. Such activities gave them more satisfaction, by their own admission, than their previous anti-social behavior.

Results for one eighth-grade class, taken from the California Achievement Test, revealed that after one year of individualized reading all students had progressed in reading skills at least one year over the previous year. Ten students had progressed one year and six months. Four students had progressed two to three years. All students have a mental capacity of average or above average.

The El Monte teachers who have tried individualized reading agree that a good way to help children grow is to take each child where he is and supply him with a favorable social and intellectual environment that will stimulate his desire to think and produce creatively at his own level. They believe that self-selection of reading materials is one way to achieve this goal.

If you should ask one of these teachers what to do with a class that was bored, restless, and not achieving up to expectancy, you should not be surprised if he said, "Why not try self-selection?"

## BIBLIOGRAPHY

*The Educational Trend* #654, Veatch, J., "Individualized Reading —For Success in the Classroom." 1954, Arthur C. Croft Publication.

Garrettson, Grace, "How One School Read the Needs of the Slow Learner." *Claremont Reading Conference,* 19th Yearbook, Calif., Claremont College Reading Laboratory, 1954.

Jenkins, Marian, "Here's to Success in Reading—Self-selection Helps" *Childhood Education,* Nov., 1955.

Kuder, G. Frederic, and Paulson, Blanche B., Better Living Booklets, *Exploring Children's Interests.* S.R.A. 1951.

Olson, Willard, "Seeking, Self-selection, and Pacing in the Use of Books by Children," The Packet, Vol. 7, No. 1 Spring 1952, Boston: D. C. Heath, pp. 3-10.

Palmer, Delores Cooper, *To Determine the Reaction of a Fourth Grade to a Program of Self-selection of Reading Materials.* Unpublished master's thesis, Salt Lake City, University of Utah, 1953. Director of Research, Marie M. Hughes, Chap. VI, "Theoretical Considerations Underlying a Program of Self-selection in Reading with Recommendations."

Robinson, Helen, "What Research Says to the Teacher of Reading, Reading Interests"—*The Reading Teacher,* Feb. 1955, pp. 173-191.

Witty, Paul, "Improving Reading Interests and Independent Reading." Promoting Maximal Reading Growth Among Able Learners, p. 141, Supplementary Educ. Monographs No. 81, Chicago: Univ. of Chicago Press, 1954.

Chapter

# 11.

## STOP READING IN
## ABILITY GROUPS

*Harriett Wilson,*
*Helping Teacher,*
*Public Schools,*
*Tucson, Arizona*

*Miss Wilson emphasizes how self-selection encour-*
*ages richness in learning and how grouping can be*
*done on other than ability basis.*

FOR MANY YEARS, I was quite convinced that dividing children into ability groups was essential for teaching children to read. Though I was often disappointed about the progress made by some of my children, I didn't believe that adjustment to individual differences could be made unless a major portion of the reading program was based on a carefully organized ability-grouping plan. However, new insights about how learning takes place, and a keen desire to improve my results, caused me to try other ways of helping children learn to read. I am now happy to report a large measure of success through individualized ways of teaching reading.

### How the Change Came About

Regardless of how tactful or clever I was in handling ability groups, I know that many parents and children experienced a considerable amount of anxiety because of my stereotyped

From *The Instructor,* April, 1956. Copyrighted by F. A. Owen Publishing Company and used by permission.

method (as I see it now) of trying to group children according to ability. It caused anxiety in many children and was in many ways a handicap to learning to read. There was of course the thrill for the child who managed to progress upward to a more advanced group, but there was also the discouragement of the slow learner or the late developer who felt quite sure that he would never get beyond belonging to a slow group.

I began to ask myself questions. Is a child likely to accept himself as a worthy person if his parents, his peers, and his teachers think of him as someone in the "dumb group"? Is he likely to develop into a self-confident and capable individual in an atmosphere where the boundaries for his learning become somewhat "set"?

According to my interpretation of recent research findings, children tend to accept themselves more readily when they feel a measure of success as they work toward goals that are realistic for them. Self-acceptance fosters acceptance of others and contributes to wholesome living for all those who are affected. When self-confidence and self-respect are not seriously threatened, most children learn to read; and greater achievement is assured when individual differences are met in ways that take advantage of the many resources which differences provide. Individualized ways of teaching reading help to do this.

I believe that emphasis on ability grouping tends to set boundaries for learning that are difficult to break. I try now to provide an environment in which each child, with my help and the resources which the other children can provide, can achieve on his own level without being limited by the boundaries which ability-grouping plans so often impose.

## What Are Individualized Ways?

It should be explained at the outset that individualized ways of teaching reading do not eliminate groups. There may be many groups in individualized plans, but they are centered around a variety of needs and purposes rather than around ability to learn. Groups based on interests, jobs to be done, and friendship are examples. In some instances children with similar difficulties may for a time work together, but I try hard not to do anything which might cause children to feel that they "belong" to either fast, slow, or average ability groups. Of course children naturally recognize that there are differences in ability and I see no reason for trying to hide the fact from them, but I don't think it is necessary to capitalize on these differences in ways which reward or punish what we think of as ability to learn.

"But just how do you go about teaching children to read by individualized ways?" teachers ask. From my experience as one teacher who gradually changed over, I can relate some situations which emerged for me. First of all, I find that a rich classroom environment is necessary. Many carefully selected books, many interest centers, and the use of every opportunity where reading meets a need are essential. The teacher should be alert, radiating a high degree of interest and maintaining that high interest. With little encouragement children will come armed with insects, rocks, shells, with scraps of this-and-that. Whatever they are, a good teacher seizes the opportunities which they present and uses them to foster more learning. Reading is one of the tools.

Some teachers ask, "But how do you have time for individualized reading?" My answer is, "I have not found that it takes more time than ability-grouping plans. However, it involves a different use of time and a more satisfactory use of children's time. I spend approximately the same amount of my time helping each individual as I did when I had ability groups."

At one time my third-graders were patiently watching the

slow metamorphosis of tadpoles over a three-month period and at the same time were maintaining a desert terrarium inhabited by a series of lizards and horned toads. The group soon developed an attitude of "look it up," to find out about their treasures. An attitude of research to find the facts, and a belief that books provide a place to find answers, emerged.

The children found great satisfaction in being able to locate information. If a child found a book that was difficult for him to read he quite often asked some friends who could help him. By working on the task together these children were able to present a good report to the class. A kind of grouping was needed for this experience. The child who encountered difficulty called upon his friends for help. He not only selected the reading material he wanted, but had a part in selecting his group. This kind of grouping makes a wonderful working "togetherness" and helps to provide a happy, purposeful situation for the learners. Meaningful communication takes place within the group, reports are given to the class, discussion ensues, stories and letters are often written, pictures and murals are painted.

As a child works, whether he is a fast or a slow learner, with the teacher's encouragement and guidance, he reads what he is able to read, and quite often shares his findings with others. Many of his reading experiences are accompanied by other kinds of experiences in the use of a variety of tools. When he writes he also spells and reads. The teacher helps him learn phonics and other word-attack methods that aid in deciphering new words.

An essential aspect of individualized reading is the emphasis on children's literature. Many good books on a wide range of reading levels and interests are provided. Many are read carefully and shared.

Joseph Krumgold's Newbery prize winner, . . . *and Now*

*Miguel,* a story about a twelve-year-old boy from the Southwest, had strong appeal for my third-graders. All of my children last year enjoyed it through reading it themselves, or listening to others as they read it orally. It was well digested, discussed, and enjoyed to the hilt. With sensitivity, the children understood Miguel and his problems of human relations and, best of all, this story seemed to help them understand and accept themselves better. Letters to the author and publisher provided exciting experiences for the children and answers to their letters were highly prized.

Through experiences such as these, children acquire a deep love and high regard for good books. A priceless attitude toward reading is built. The slow reader is gaining something that is even more valuable than a "basic vocabulary." He is becoming convinced that books are wonderful things! Eventually, though for some not until they reach the upper grades, they learn to read better and usually without humiliation and without pain.

In my opinion, individualized reading plans provide many rich opportunities to help children make the best of their abilities and resources. There are few limits to bind them if the environment is rich with opportunities to read, to communicate and share with an appreciative audience what they learn.

Another source for our reading experiences in third grade last year was magazines and the newspaper. Children would report the morning temperature and gradually they became aware of headlines concerning the President, his grandchildren, and other items of special interest. We avidly followed the antics of "George L. Mountainlion" who wrote a column in the Sunday paper concerning the local museum which we visited. Before long all the children cherished the honor of reading the column to the class on Monday morning. Third-graders were acquiring the newspaper habit.

Bringing in informed people is another source of stimulation and knowledge. One child's father, a modest but world-recognized ornithologist, who enthralled the children with his bird lore, set the class off on a long chain of events. A university student from Holland told the children about Christmas in Holland.

I took advantage of almost everything that happened. When the street near our school was being paved, we arranged for one child to operate the pneumatic drill. This led to simple science experiments about air compression and to many other experiences which involved reading as well as other learning situations.

An interesting observation occurred in the first experiences of the children in their new approach to reading. Someone often asked, "When are we going to read?" Eventually, however, they were helped to understand that the news we wrote on the board was reading, that the "look it up" experiences were reading, that the child who laboriously wrote an experience chart on large-sized paper with a marking pen was reading, and that enjoying storybooks was reading. For some reason, it took a little time to understand that learning to read didn't have to take place in the traditional three-group reading situation.

What evidence can I show that individualized reading is effective? The fourth-grade teacher tells me that my children's attitudes toward research, their skills in critical thinking, their sharp evaluations, their creativity, and their poise and ability to express themselves are excitingly apparent! She finds them amazingly aware of authors and books. They know Ann Nolan Clark. Robert McCloskey is an old friend. Ludwig Bemelmans' *Parsley* is greeted with cheers. In addition, standardized test results show more than normal growth in reading skills.

I don't say that individualized reading is the only way or

that ability grouping is the wrong way. More experimentation and research are probably needed to provide conclusive answers. But, in my opinion, individualized reading, though much of it is done through group situations, is an effective way of helping children learn to read. It helps to free children for creative and meaningful reading in accordance with their abilities to give and to receive. Differences in ability are used to help provide a wide range of resources, increasing opportunities for all to do their best.

# AN INDIVIDUAL PROGRAM
# OF READING

*Phyllis Parkin, Principal, Eastern Parkway School,*
*State College, Pennsylvania*

> *Mrs. Parkin relates her experience in fourth grade*
> *with an individualized approach. This article contains*
> *some fine descriptions of how she proceeded, what she*
> *found helpful, and how she was better able to meet*
> *the wide range of differences in her class than under*
> *previous reading procedures.*

IN JUNE, A GROUP of 36 eight- and nine-year-olds, labeled "Fourth Grade," completed a year's program in reading under a highly individualized method. The children, who had been introduced to the program the previous September, took to it like the proverbial ducks to water. The boys and girls read eagerly and prodigiously. They read for fun; they read for information. They read alone; they read together. Most of the pupils chose wisely and read widely. (One girl read 147 books.) They grew in their ability to have fun, find information, weigh comparisons, and draw conclusions. In short, they learned to make good use of what they read. Their reading was dynamic and functional.

When these boys and girls were asked which they liked better, group reading or individual reading, their reply came in a chorus, "Individual!"

The next query, "Why?" brought the following comments:

From *Educational Leadership*, October 1956. Used by permission.

"I like individual reading because I can choose any book I want to read."

"I like this kind of reading because I can read as fast as I want to."

"Last year, everybody knew I was in the second reading group until I got good enough to move into the highest one. This year, no one knows what group I'm in because there aren't any groups!" (This conclusion was accompanied by a smile of satisfaction.)

"I like individual reading especially because I don't have to wait for anyone else to finish a story before I can go on to a new one."

"This kind of reading is more fun because I can find out what I want to for myself. I don't have to answer questions that someone else makes up."

"I like individual reading because the teacher doesn't pass out books and say, 'Today we're going to begin to read this book together.' "

"The reason I'd rather have individual reading is because I can ask a friend to read with me or I can read alone if I'd rather."

"I like to hear about all the books the others are reading. That helps me to choose my next book sometimes."

"In this kind of reading, the teacher just helps those who need help. The rest of us don't have to learn over again what we already know."

If only these thrilling testimonials had been caught on a tape to preserve the conviction and the excitement in the young voices! Many teachers and supervisors considering an individualized reading program seem to feel that these benefits mentioned by the children ought to result. Doubts often come pouring into their minds, however, to water the courage it takes to launch such a program. Here, "out of the mouths of babes," tumble words of sincere testimonial that should give them courage.

## What Is Needed?

Just what is needed to start an individualized reading program? First, *children* who want to read better and a *teacher* who wants to teach them to read by the best method she can devise. The teacher should be willing to give the individualized plan of reading a fair trial with her children. Although the children will be happy for such an adventure, the teacher may be bothered by the uncertain feeling of not knowing all the answers in advance. There is no set pattern to follow; she must work one out as she goes. But she should have no fears. The children will help the teacher even as she helps them.

A second "must" is a supervisor who approves and encourages the teacher in undertaking this kind of program. The teacher probably has not used this method before. There is no teachers' manual to follow. The program, at least at the beginning, is bound to be of an experimental nature. The teacher's greatest asset is an understanding person who can help her evaluate the progress she is making under the new plan, whether this person be principal, supervisor or administrator.

In the third place, a wide variety of reading materials must be available. This factor alone may make or break the adventure into individualized reading. In all probability, there will be on hand basal texts, supplementary readers and library books. In addition, assiduous use must be made of the public library, the bookmobile, of every possible source of books in the community. Parents, too, are usually willing to allow their children to share their books at school. Five books per child is perhaps a rough estimate for which to aim. These should range in difficulty according to the spread of abilities in the group of children using them. The assortment will include, in addition to those mentioned before, texts in the various subject matter areas such as social studies and science as well as numerous story books, easy and difficult, just for fun. There must be something to tickle every one's taste. The selections should be changed from time to time with care being taken to retain those that some children are still looking forward to reading. At the time of change, books may be found to satisfy the particular needs or choices of certain children. As we well know, some children will read anything but some are "choosey" and it is the teacher's job to satisfy them all, while at the same time she is trying to help the fussy child broaden his reading horizon.

## How to Begin

With teacher, children and supervisor in the mood, and with a reasonably good supply of books of varying difficulty and diverse interests, how shall the program be initiated? This is perhaps the most imposing barrier of all. Once hurdled, however, it soon shrinks away to nothing.

There is no right or wrong pattern. Here is the way one teacher did it. At the very beginning of the year, before any type of program was under way, she told the children that this year reading was going to be a little different. She explained that there would be no reading groups as such and that each person would choose his own book and read it as he was able. She talked with the pupils about choosing carefully and planning to finish the book begun. She also told them not to scorn a book that looked easy because in doing so they might cheat themselves out of a good story. (This suggestion was made with the idea of lifting pressure from the slow reader who needed to choose an easy book to read.)

The teacher further explained that, instead of calling groups of children to read with her every day, she would stop by to talk with each child about the book he was reading or to ask him to read to her. She would always be present to answer questions or to help in finding a book. From time to time, she would bring together children who needed the same kind of help and work with them in a group; this group would not remain the same, though, from one day to the next.

She asked the children if they thought it would be a good idea to keep a list of the books they had to read so that at the end of the year they could see what they had accomplished in reading. The boys and girls agreed and decided that this list should contain the title of the book, its author, and just a brief summary or comment about the content.

By way of pulling together this plan and setting the project in motion, the teacher asked, "From our discussion this morning, what different things do you see that you might be doing during our reading time?" As the children replied, she wrote on the board:

1. *Choose a book to read.*
2. *Read.*
3. *List the book in your notebook.*

If a child already had a book to read at his desk, then he had no reason for going to the shelves for another. Other children, however, went a few at a time to select a book to read. On that initial day, a majority of the children settled soon to serious reading. A few were restless, however, and needed help in choosing something suited to their interests and abilities. One child simply could not find anything he liked. Here was a challenge for the teacher, to find the right story for the "choosey" child.

Perhaps no child would be ready, the teacher thought, to list a book completed on the first day. On the contrary, several rapid readers chose attractively packaged "easy" books and had several to list during the very first period.

As the year went on, teacher and children found other activities that belonged in the reading period. One by one, the following were added:

4. *Read together.*

This came to mean one of two things: either two or three children sat together just for the sake of companionship, each reading his own book; or two or more children read together from the same books by taking turns reading orally or by "playing parts."

5. *List new words and their meanings.*

The word list and functional use of the dictionary developed naturally from the often-asked question, "What does this word mean?" The readers of more advanced material began this phase of their reading earlier in the year and, of course, went much further with it than the slower readers. Some children became fascinated with words and spent a good deal of time in word study.

6. *Share the books you read.*

By this, the children meant describing a particular book to their classmates. A favorite method was that of telling an exciting adventure or leading up to a point of suspense in the story so that half a dozen children would be begging, "May I have the book next?"

Another trick the children developed was to describe an incident or a character and ask if anyone could identify the book from the description. Some children gave a brief oral review so that a child seeking a particular type of book could tell whether this suited his taste.

Some very fine experiences in story telling, building suspense, summarizing important points, and in listening came out of this phase of the reading.

7. *Do something with what you read.*

Sometimes a story or a part of a story offered excellent material for dramatization and a child would take charge of a group for such a project.

Many times the book being read had information needed for a report or for use in other ways. Gerald needed tracing paper to get the pattern for a simple wagon he found described in a make-it-yourself book. Then he took down the directions to use at home. Diane drew illustrations of incidents or scenes that stirred her. Donny loved birds and took down information he wanted to put in his illustrated bird book. Dennis would tolerate nothing but trains for a while and he listed certain facts he wanted to keep. April and Susan found a vivid description of an oasis which impressed them so they transformed the word description into a diorama. These youngsters and many others actually put reading to work for them.

The time set aside each day for reading grew from 25 minutes in September to more than an hour in June and often started out with a listing together of these seven activities. These seldom appeared in the same order but each child would be engaged in one activity depending upon which stage he had reached at the time. One item never came out on the list, perhaps because it was simply taken for granted: *Get help from the teacher.*

An individualized reading program provides a very great advantage. Children learn to read by reading. In this program, therefore, each child can do something about his own reading during all the time set aside for reading. He is also at liberty to continue his progress in any free time he has at home or at school.

### Teacher's Responsibility

It is obvious that in this type of program there is a shift in emphasis in the teacher's responsibility. Instead of calling a group of children around her so that she may teach them all the same thing whether they need it or not, her duties are somewhat different. She must know what books are on the shelves and she must know enough of their contents so that she will be able to advise the children in making their selections.

She must never lack the time to encourage and actually teach the slow worker. She must never fail to inspire the gifted reader to more effective use of his reading potential. Phonics is not omitted from this type of reading program but it is given only as it is needed, not as a routine procedure for everybody. Each day, the teacher should work with as many children as possible, talking with them, reading with them, noting their difficulties. From time to time, she will group those with similar needs for specific help. Actually, she does all the kinds of teaching she would do under the group system but only for the pupils who need such help. Thus the teacher can permit other pupils to go in their reading, never stopping until they get tired or come to some situation they are unable to handle alone.

## Evaluation of Learning

How can a teacher ascertain whether her children are learning to read better by this method? This seems to be the chief concern of those who are considering a more individualized approach.

In the first place, the teacher need not be too concerned, for example, about the nine-year-olds who are reading from the short stories of Oscar Wilde and *The Story of Fission,* except perhaps to ask, "Am I providing them with plenty of stimulating reading material?"

Then, there are certain gains she cannot help observing: freedom of choice and the joy that accompanies it; release from the tethering gait of the group; release from the stigma of the group label; a relaxed attitude toward reading; the pleasure of making reading a live, dynamic activity; more time for reading for the purposes that reading can serve; a change of emphasis from competition with the group to competition with one's self.

Sheer number of books read is some indication of the child's accomplishment although length of list alone is no proof of growth. If the difficulty of the last book read is the same as that of the first, little growth may have taken place. But if a considerable number of books has been read, some growth must surely have happened, and one measurement of progress may lie in a comparison of the reading levels of the first and the last books.

If a child reads nothing but dog stories, for example, at the beginning of the year and, toward the end, selects a narrative of family life or an adventure or science-fiction, then surely growth has taken place.

If actual scholastic achievement must be the measure of gain, a teacher can get this by giving a good standardized achievement test in reading at the beginning of the year and then again at the end. The one given at the beginning of the year can serve two purposes; it can be a guide to point up the learning-gaps she should be on the watch for in certain boys and girls; it can also indicate the range of abilities for which she must provide books. Measurement of growth is better shown through comparing what a child is reading with what he was reading than in determining how he surpasses other children in his group or those in another group.

If a teacher feels she must know whether her children have made progress comparable with that which might have been theirs through use of a set of basal readers, she may want to try to make use of some of the measuring devices which are provided for such readers.

For a teacher who is more concerned with the child than the subject, who prefers the personal rather than the mass approach, who sees value in stressing, not regimentation, but growth and development, a more individualized approach to reading, such as described in this article, may be a step in the right direction.

Chapter

# 13.

## YOU CAN INDIVIDUALIZE YOUR READING PROGRAM, TOO

*Mary Ann Daniel, Fifth Grade Teacher, Highland School, Abingdon, Pennsylvania.*

*This article is particularly helpful in describing how book supply was increased, how children kept a reading "diary," and how their interest in reading developed.*

RECENTLY MANY articles have been written stressing the effectiveness of individualized reading programs. I became as enthusiastic as anyone else who has read these articles—here at last was a method which could cope with the wide range of reading abilities within a classroom. The best way to meet individual differences is to deal with them individually. Now, my classroom was going to be different! Reading was going to be fun! All of my pupils were going to read and like it, I hoped.

As I gazed at the 36 faces—some eager, some apprehensive —on the first day of school in September, I wondered if my plan would succeed. It sounded perfect in every article I had read. But 36 fifth grade youngsters! My school district, in a rather well-to-do suburb of Philadelphia, believes in grouping for reading. Almost every classroom in our eleven elementary schools has three reading groups. This year, a new reading series was purchased which encouraged the ability grouping.

From *Elementary English*, November, 1956. Used by permission of author and publisher.

The size of my class and the policy of the school district would certainly encourage the "old-fashioned" ability grouping!

I was determined to make an attempt to work out a plan for a combination—group and individualized reading program. The first thing I did was to check the reading ability level of all of the children. This was done for grouping and for my beginning records for the individualized reading. Each child read a paragraph from a story, we talked about it briefly, and we also talked of how they felt about reading in general. It was both amazing and discouraging to discover the number of children who responded, "I hate it, I can't read."

We had our regular reading groups. I gradually worked out the policy, for the top group first, that one day a week they could read any book they selected during a reading period. I checked what they read individually that day. The other two groups responded, just as I hoped they would, by demanding to know why they couldn't read a book of their own choice also. Soon everyone was making this own selection from our room library of approximately 150-200 books.

From there it was easy to guide the children into forming a Book Club. The first undertaking of the club was a book exchange. Books were brought from home—sometimes six or eight at a time by one youngster. The books were all excellent ones! Only one child brought in a comic book, and the youngsters themselves decided they didn't want any more! The first president of the club, who was an extremely capable little girl, planned programs for the care and handling of books, book quizzes, rearranging and classifying the library shelves (the fifth grade star football player took charge of this task), and getting others interested in reading. From this last topic they decided to present book reviews at least once a week. At first our book reviews were merely short resumes. The more imaginative youngsters later presented drawings, puppet shows, and short plays. These activities took place during a regular reading period or in the afternoon. Much of the time formerly spent on workbooks was being devoted to these creative activities. Our workbook exercises still got done, however!

Reading periods, when we had the individualized program, always ran 40 to 60 minutes. This was never too much time; in fact, the majority of the children requested more time. During that time I called individuals, volunteers first, over to a corner where we talked about what had happened in the book thus far, discussed the characters and their actions, made predictions of what was to come, read a paragraph orally, and discussed how the book had helped them as individuals. Any difficulties the child had were noted, and later they were worked on. If there was a common problem for five or six youngsters, we went over it together. Individual problems were naturally taken care of individually without wasting the time of the entire group. I found that with my weakest students, who had a great deal of difficulty, it was easier to give them individual assistance either before or after school.

The children kept a diary of the books they read. They made a very short comment about each book, told whether they liked it or not, and discussed what they gained from having read the book. I might say the last two items were the most difficult for them. They could not understand, at first, that it was permissible to say they did not like a book. All of the children thought they *had* to say they liked every book they read. Many of them did not understand what was meant by, "How did the book help you become a better individual?" We had several discussions on this, and more and more of them gradually included that item in their diaries. I found that short book reviews of this type were a help in finding books they would like to receive for Christmas. Brief resumes were written about the most appealing books; these were typed and mimeographed and sent home for Christmas suggestions. After reading several books, the children were encouraged to write their own stories. These were put into book form—bound and illustrated—instead of just written on "good penmanship paper." These books were kept in a conspicuous place so that they were available for reading at all times. What could thrill a child more than to see someone pick up his "bound book" to read?

Of course the time for telling about a book read is most valuable. It is amazing to watch the methods of presentation change and improve as the children do more and more of this reporting. At first all of the reports seemed to follow the same pattern: "This book was about. . . . If you want to know what happened read it." I thought to myself, "Where is all the creativity that is supposed to develop in this reading program?" An original presentation by just one youngster was all that was needed to inspire the others. Soon we had radio reporters, plays, pictures, drawings on the blackboard, papier mache puppets, string puppets, and book reviews written in our classroom newspaper. The more creative the presentation, the more irresistible the book became to the other youngsters.

As this program was going on, I still had my regular groups about three days a week. The creativeness from the individual program carried over to the groups. We did more dramatization and felt freer to skip around in the book and select stories that had a particular interest at that time instead of reading from the first story to the last in the correct sequence. I have found that all of the children, in the group reading and individually, felt much freer to come to me for assistance. While working in groups, instead of waiting for everyone to finish, those finished first worked on their book diaries or methods of presenting books read.

As I have watched this reading program develop since September, I have been most pleased with its results. It has enabled me to know more about the level and ability of each child. Thus I have been able to give more worth-while individual and group assistance. Naturally, as the children read more books, they become more skilled in self selection of books. They are very capable of selecting books that they understand and that are well-written. The weaker pupils are not embarrassed by their selection of easier books, and the superior readers are not held back. Everyone exhibits more enthusiasm and interest in reading. Because the slower readers select books they are able to read, they soon develop confidence in their reading ability, and their whole attitude towards reading is changed. In the individual program the children want to read; the more they read, the greater degree of success they feel in all of their school work.

# SELF-SELECTION IN READING

*Marian Jenkins, Curriculum Consultant in Elementary Education, Los Angeles County, California*

*Mrs. Jenkins describes the experiences of principals and teachers as they proceeded to develop a reading program to meet the needs of individual children. She includes a detailed description of one of the best experimental studies presently available.*

HERE IS A REPORT of three principals in whose whose elementary schools reading is becoming a successful venture for more and more boys and girls and where children's reading, as far as parents are concerned, is becoming less of a worry and more of a joy. These teachers are using self-selection as the way of learning to read printed materials. The story for them began with the study of the findings of Willard Olson, who recognizes that all learning is really a process of self-selection. The learner is continuously seeking from the environment and selecting the experiences which meet his need at a particular moment. For example, as his need for food, sleep or affection is met, he grows. As those in the environment provide the learner with materials, situations, encouragement and approval, he continues to develop. Through their care for him and their planning for situations which will provide the condi-

From *The Reading Teacher,* December, 1957. Used by permission of the author and publisher.

tions for growth, Olson says, they pace the learner's seeking and selecting.

## Self-selection and Academic Learning

When this theory is applied to academic learning the same behavior on the part of the learner is exhibited. With the guidance of people who care and offer opportunity for the learner to select, he learns with confidence, with success and with a growing sense of personal achievement. This theory though well established and documented has not been widely applied to reading. However, reports of self-selection in reading published in this journal, in *Childhood Education, Elementary English,* and other periodicals are growing in number. More and more teachers are welcoming procedures which do away with the deleterious effects of labeling the less able and of permitting the more able to achieve to only a minimum of their possibilities. So self-selection in reading is becoming an important consideration to those who first look at the child and his ways of learning and then design procedure that will pace him in seeking and selecting that which satisfies his needs. What are the essentials for self-selection in reading? One essential is books and more books—books from school, city and county collections, from children's and teachers' personal libraries and magazines, newspapers and other printed materials. Books on every subject—both textbooks and trade books of many levels of reading difficulty are needed.

Next is needed a thoughtfully planned organization in which each child may browse and choose his own reading material, may talk over his choice with interested friends, which includes the teacher, and then may have considerable time to read and read. No waiting for another to finish for his turn to come, no listening to another's halting progress, no need to fuss about the place when his turn does come. He chose the book, he therefore wants to read it, and he does.

Most important is the time the teacher gives to the individual —listening to him read, conferring about his progress, helping him with every type of skill as he reads it, encouraging him and laying plans with him for next steps. The teacher and child may keep a record together or separately. An effective record includes titles of books, dates when a book was chosen and completed, dates of conferences, notes on problems met and progress in skills, comprehension and also appreciation. A record should also tell how the child planned to report his reading. Some books are of such high interest and importance to him, the science experiments which result from reading so exciting to the class, dramatizations so much fun, puppet shows such attractions—that great variety in ways of sharing individual interests and achievement in reading are created.

Let the principals tell their own stories!

Frances Cyrog, Principal, Lou Henry Hoover School, Whittier Elementary School District, California, opens her discussion with these quotes:

> "For the first time I believe I am teaching reading in accordance with my knowledge of the way children grow and develop."
>
> "This is a reading program which has no quarrel with what we know about how children learn."
>
> "For any teacher truly interested in meeting individual needs self-selection in reading is the answer!"

These are teachers speaking after two years of using self-selection in reading throughout the six grades of one elementary school. Several had begun the previous year when a group of experienced teachers, consultants and principals were introduced to this way of teaching reading in a series of meetings planned by a Los Angeles County Curriculum Consultant, and

the Whittier Assistant Superintendent in charge of Curriculum.
The first and second grade teachers were among this group and
we returned to school excited about the possibilities of such a
reading program.

### Teachers Use New Ideas

We discussed the ideas presented and started our adventure.
That first year was one of continuous discovery because we
were able to talk together often, call on resource people freely,
and have access to the latest research. We received help with
our problems, answers to our questions and always encouragement and support. Slowly and with careful planning we moved
into this reading program which held so much promise.

The evidence from our records built up, children and parents
showed enthusiasm and our further study together encouraged
the upper grade teachers to introduce self-selection the following year.

### Reviewing Progress Made

Now, two years later, we have additional information to
support the program which appeared so promising.

Keeping parents informed proved to be a vital part of the
program. They must know, we felt sure, that in using this
technique, we could keep better records than ever before on
comprehension, on word attack skills, on growth in vocabulary,
and, most important of all, children's response to and satisfaction in reading. And, certainly, we must listen to parents, too!
For they told us much about the success of the process. A repeated cause for wonder on the part of parents of primary
children was that they tackled anything in the way of print.

"My older child seemed to think reading was restricted to the
classroom and the textbook, but John reads newspapers, maga-

zines and signs in store windows. Reading is an exciting source
of information to him."

Another mother, women's page editor of our daily newspaper, had long mourned the apathy of her two daughters
toward reading. With the advent of this method in her younger
daughter's class she reported happily to the Claremont Reading
Conference:

> "This is one of the things we didn't believe could happen in
> our family. Our older girl, now in seventh grade, went through
> the group system and she didn't like reading at all. This pattern
> was repeating itself with our fifth grade daughter. Suddenly this
> year all of us thought we were seeing things when the lights
> were on in her bedroom late and she was still reading. When she
> pulled the flashlight under the blanket technique on me I was
> convinced."

And what of the children? They gave us fresh clues each day
as they revealed their ideas in such ways as these:

> "I can read what I choose—any book in our room! I like to
> tell others about my book and hear about theirs. Lots of books
> are very interesting and you might like to read their book and
> they might like to read yours."

> "Selective reading has helped me to be a better reader and
> read books that I would otherwise not have read. Books help
> me to learn about people and places I never knew."

> "In selective reading you can read different kinds of books,
> and at your own speed (slow or fast). You can stop to think
> about the things you like."

> "I think you become a better reader if you read books you
> like. If you get a dull book you don't have to keep on reading it.
> In the old way when we had readers it sometimes got very
> boring."

> "We all get to read the books we like and want to read. We
> all have the same chance to read. In reading groups the best

readers were in one group and then on down. And the ones who couldn't read as well never had a good chance."

First graders also knew why they liked self-selection. The class had used self-selection for a month and had read from ten to forty pre-primers and primers. The teacher, as an experiment, chose a group of ten children reading in what would have been a middle group. She introduced a fine and well-liked primer which they read together for two weeks. A skillful person, well schooled in ability group techniques, she carefully motivated the children and progressed according to the pattern she had used previous to beginning self-selection. When the book was finished she casually introduced a discussion about how they might like to read their next book. The response was immediate. A student-teacher recorded the discussion. The many favorable remarks ran like this:

Mike: "I like to read more books and I can read them faster."
Pat: "I like to choose my own book because it's more fun."
Janet: "I like choosing books better because you get to read the whole book. You don't have to stop so much."

As a principal, reflecting on these experiences, nothing has been more stimulating than the response of teachers, their careful study of the program, the many hours they have willingly given to evaluation, meeting with and teaching for visitors, keeping records, compiling test results, and bringing to children their enthusiasm. And most of all is the awareness of the growth we have all made in our understanding of children.

Antoinette McChristy, Principal, Christian Sorensen School, Whittier Elementary School District, California starts her account in this way:

"Everytime I get answers! Books even tell you how to take care of dogs!"

Second grader, Tommy, had made this exciting discovery during the self-selection reading time. Such enthusiastic remarks about books and stories are frequently overheard in classes where self-selection reading is being used.

However, at first there were certain questions in the minds of teachers and administrators concerning the use of self-selection in primary grades. Even though classrooms contained carefully chosen books, could second graders be trusted to select reading materials which would expand and refine their reading skills? Would standardized tests show that pupils using self-selection progress as well as those being taught in conventional reading groups?

The questions needed to be answered, so "A Comparative Study to Determine Whether Self-selective Reading Can Be Successfully Used at The Second Grade Level" was carried out. The research extending over a period of one year compared the reading gains made by one hundred sixty boys and girls carefully selected from eight second grade classes. In four of these classes (control group) conventional reading methods were used, while self-selection was employed in the other four (experimental group). The children in the two groups were comparable in mental age, intelligence and socio-economic background. The teachers were matched on the basis of educational training and experience.

### Arranging the Environment

Books, and more books seemed to be the keynote in the experimental classes. Prior to the actual initiation of self-selection, two or three days were spent by each teacher in setting up the classroom library. The children, with the teacher's guidance, worked out plans for the display of the reading materials. Each class developed the room environment which best suited its needs. However, one basic practice was common. The books were invitingly arranged and easily accessible to the children. Then children had time to browse and choose, each his own book.

## Grouping

It was thought that children in primary grades would feel more comfortable about their reading if they could gather around the teacher and be assured of her immediate help. In order to keep this intimate contact between the children and teacher, some sort of grouping was planned.

*The teachers using self-selection wished to avoid any grouping based upon the reading proficiency of the pupils, since this would counteract the very environment which they were striving to create. Also, more equal distribution of the teacher's assistance could be given if groups were composed of approximately equal numbers of slow, average, and fast readers. With these factors in mind, each teacher developed her own method of grouping. In general, groups were formed on the basis of friendships, common interests or common problems.*

One teacher decided to base her groups on the results of a simple sociometric test. She asked each child in a casual manner the following question: "Whom would you like most to sit near at reading time?" On the basis of the children's choices, three groups were formed. A chubby second grader explained to a visitor, "We don't have a 'dumb' group, we just read with our friends." Friendships were being strengthened and good attitudes toward reading were growing while children chuckled over the funny part of a story or helped one another with the hard words in their chosen books.

## Measuring Results of Growth in Reading Skills

The individualized groups met with the teacher on a daily basis. Each child in the group had his "special time" with the teacher for individual instruction. His particular reading problem was brought into sharp focus and reading skills were reviewed, developed and refined at the time of immediate need.

A detailed reading record card was kept for each child. Daily reference was made to this record in order to ascertain whether the difficulties of yesterday had been mastered or if they still persisted. This practice gave continuity to the instruction and kept both child and teacher aware of just what the problems were and what progress had been made.

Control groups were set up for use in comparing growth in the reading skills. In the control groups instruction was given to three groups based on reading ability. Books to be read were selected by the teachers from series available. They worked with each group each day following suggestions in the manuals. A record of books read was kept for each child. Varied related independent activities were available to the children at times when the teacher was not working directly with them and these groups also had access to well stocked classroom libraries.

The results of standardized reading tests showed that self-selection produced significantly greater gains than did conventional reading methods in the areas of reading vocabulary, reading comprehension and total reading.

The control group averaged 1.14 years in total reading gains while the experimental group averaged 1.41 years.

25% of the control group had total reading gains of more than 1.6 years, while 46% of the experimental group scored within this range.

In vocabulary growth the control group averaged 1.09 and the experimental 1.96 years. In comprehension 59% of the experimental group gained 2 years or more, while 24% of the control group scored in this range.

The study indicates that second grade pupils are able to choose, from an appropriately stocked classroom library, reading material which promotes their reading growth. Therefore, it is concluded that self-selection in reading may be used successfully at the second grade level.

Claude E. Norcross, Principal, Ladera School, Las Lomitas Elementary School District, Atherton, California tells how self-selection is functioning in his school in the paragraphs below.

The self-selection or individualized approach to the reading process has been tried by four teachers in our school during the past two years.[1] The results obtained indicate that there is enough merit in it to warrant further study and experimentation.

### Careful Planning Precedes Introduction of Self-selection

Careful plans were made by these four teachers before they introduced self-selection to their pupils. Their plans included: Studying what has been written regarding it in the literature; preparing charts of comprehension and word attack skills to be developed; arranging for a large classroom collection of reading textbooks with a wide range of difficulty; arranging to have a large collection of trade books of many types and subjects and of a wide range of difficulty; preparing a plan for recording detailed information for each child concerning skill development, vocabulary development, and books read; outlining how self-selection would be introduced to the pupils and to the parents; and selecting and organizing practice materials.

With this careful preparation, each teacher was ready to introduce the new approach with the assurance that he would be conducting a systematic and comprehensive program of instruction in reading which would differ in two main ways from our regular program. First, the children would be permitted to select their own reading materials rather than follow the basic series textbooks.

[1] Mrs. Eleanor Cannon, Mrs. Mary Largent, Mr. Robert Newman, and Mr. Thomas Price, Ladera School, Las Lomitas School District, Atherton, California.

Second, the skills program would be developed primarily on an individual basis rather than within the three customary ability groups.

## Reports to the Staff Are Essential

The teachers using self-selection in reading instruction have periodically reported to the entire staff on the methods and the results obtained. We feel that this is an essential step in any special program devised to test the effectiveness of new methods of instruction.

## The Program Is Evaluated

During the past two years six classes, approximately one hundred forty children in grades three through six, have participated in self-selection in reading under the direction of four teachers. An analysis of the results obtained from achievement tests administered to the two classes participating in this program during the 1955-56 school year indicate that the pupils made slightly, though not significantly, more progress in skill development than pupils in the regular program. Test results for the four classes that participated during the 1956-57 school year are not yet available. However, it is in the evaluation of progress toward other important objectives of reading instruction where self-selection has been most effective. The children who have participated in self-selection seem to have developed an abiding interest in reading, found keen enjoyment in it, developed the ability to select suitable materials for reading, and above all have developed the habit of reading beyond that which has been achieved in our regular program.

The teachers who have participated in self-selection have reported a new thrill in teaching reading. They, like the children, seem to have found a new interest in children's literature.

# INDIVIDUALIZED READING:
# A PROGRAM OF SEEKING,
# SELF-SELECTION, AND PACING

*May Lazar, Assistant Director, Bureau of Educational Research, Board of Education of the City of New York*

*Dr. Lazar presents a comprehensive view of an individual approach to the teaching of reading. She describes the thinking which resulted in experimentation in the New York City schools and discusses some of the results as the project proceeded.*

READING HAS BEEN for many years and still is perhaps the topic most frequently discussed by teachers, supervisors, and specialists. The development of effective reading programs has probably been studied more often by educational research workers than any other area. In spite of this emphasis, we do not yet seem to have all the answers because we go on searching for *the* "magic formula" that will solve all reading problems for all children.

As a result of our own various research studies through the years, we had realized for some time that, while the philosophy concerning reading was in consonance with the newer thoughts on child development and learning, the practices in large measure were not. Too close adherence to grade level standards and the use of graded textbooks, which assumed that all children

Speech delivered at 1957 Conference of International Reading Association, New York City. Used by permission of the author and the International Reading Association.

move at the same pace, prevented our practices from being as forward-looking as our ideas. We began to question the slavish adherence to the *basic reader systems*. (The "sober" books as Josette Frank calls them.) There was strong belief that the materials would do the teaching rather than the teacher. There was too much confusion between methods and materials; between methods and class organization. There was also too much thinking in terms of mechanics rather than in terms of objectives and values.

We began, therefore, to "sharpen" our thoughts in view of our findings and to take a new look at the whole program—the place of reading in the total curriculum, the materials and methods used, and the results in terms of larger values rather than in terms of the skills alone. In short, were the practices and approaches meeting specifically the needs and interests of the children? What type of program would really touch the children and make them want to read and love to read?

Our belief was and still is that reading is a "way of life" and not a skills gadget-collecting procedure. To quote various authorities, this same idea has been referred to as: "unrelated bits of bric a brac"; "all children progress together bit by bit"; "we put our children on a conveyor belt of mechanics"; "we think of the teacher as a technician with a multitude of tricks."

We believe that experiences and relationships are closely related to reading activities and that reading is a vital part of the child's full life. We believe that the skills are necessary in any program, but that they must be introduced functionally. The child should know what skills he needs and *why* he needs them. The specific skills to be taught and when to teach them depends upon the strength of purposes and urgency of needs. In other words, we believe in fitting the skills to the child and not the child to the skills.

The last few years have seen the beginning of experimentation with a dynamic approach to reading evolving from an evaluation of present procedures. This approach has been referred to as "Individualized Reading." The term "approach" is here considered not as a *single method or technique* but as a *way of thinking about reading*—an attitude toward reading. Individualized Reading is based on thinking which involves new concepts, not only with respect to class organization, techniques, and materials, but also to the child's development needs as well.

In our research projects over the years, we found that it was not unusual for many classes to have a wide range of abilities from nonreaders to those who were about two years advanced. With such a situation, it was impossible to succeed with class or even group instruction. The solution seemed to lie in a truly individualized approach to reading—one that would reach the varying needs, interests, and drives of the children in the class. For several years various adaptations of this approach were tried in certain of the schools.

As we worked more and more with the individualized approach, we began to crystallize our thinking and organize and record our thoughts. Thus a tentative mimeographed brochure, *Thinking About Individualized Reading,* emerged.

During the years when the individualized approach to reading was occupying our thoughts, we found from the professional literature that others had also been working and thinking along the same lines for some time—Marian Jenkins and Grace Garrettson in California, Jeannette Veatch in Maryland, and a number of others—too numerous to list here. Willard C. Olson's studies concerned with the nature of growth, behavior, and achievement led to the concepts of *seeking, self-selection,* and *pacing.* Dr. Olson [1] points out that the healthy child is con-

[1] Willard C. Olson, "Seeking, Self-selection, and Pacing in the Use of Books by Children," *The Packet,* (Spring 1952), 3-10. Boston 16, Mass.: D. C. Heath and Company, 285 Columbus Avenue.

tinually exploring his environment and seeking experiences which fit in with his growth and needs. These seeking tendencies and self-selection of stimulating material in the environment are basic for learning. Pacing is the teacher's responsibility for providing each child with the materials and experiences at a tempo that insures success at his stage of maturity. Dr. Olson ties up these concepts admirably with the reading program. These studies gave reassurances to our own theories of Individualized Reading. Jeannette Veatch reinforces this by her definition of Individualized Reading: "An individualized reading program provides each child with an environment which allows him to seek that which stimulates him, choose that which helps him develop most, and work at his own rate regardless of what else is going on. Seeking, self-selection, and pacing (which Willard C. Olson had so well pointed out) are the concepts that give individualized reading its unusual quality." [2]

Before explaining the operation of this approach, it seems necessary to present some underlying fundamental premises, as follows:

Reading is a matter individual to each child.

A child should have the opportunity to proceed at his own pace.

The reading experiences should eliminate comparisons with others, thus minimizing feelings of inadequacy.

The level of the reader or reading material should be subordinate to the act and enjoyment of reading itself.

Allowing a child some freedom of choice in selection of his reading materials will develop real purpose for reading.

Instruction in reading and reading itself are constantly interwoven.

[2] Jeannette Veatch, "Individualized Reading—For Success in the Classroom," *The Educational Trend*, 1954. Washington 6, D. C.: Arthur C. Croft Publications, Dupont Circle Building.

If we really believe in individual differences in children, we must deal with them individually. Individualized Reading actually provides the child with the procedures he specifically needs. These may be quite different from those needed by other children in the same class.

Various names have been suggested for this approach to reading, but none seems entirely adequate. The term "Individualized Reading" is not altogether satisfactory. Some persons interpret it to mean that there is never opportunity for group or class teaching and sharing. This is completely erroneous. "Personalized Reading" and "Self-selection Reading" are also not entirely descriptive terms because they give the impression that assigned reading activities may not be included. This is also erroneous. For want of a truly descriptive term, to simplify the discussion, and because most reading authorities use this term, the title "Individualized Reading" will be used throughout this paper. Actually it is an error to place any specific name to the reading program. Individualized Reading is really the developmental approach to reading based closely on the specific capacities and needs of children and how they learn.

You have all heard of extensive, library, recreational, or independent reading. These may or may not include self-selection, but they definitely do not involve actual reading instruction as does Individualized Reading. It is generally assumed that the above four types of reading are adjuncts to the basic program going on, and that they are distinct and discrete from each other. Individualized Reading is not subordinate to or an adjunct of the basic reading program—*it is the basic program*. It is a way of organizing the class, the materials, and the individual children in order to meet the real objectives and values concerned with their learning.

The major features of Individualized Reading are that children generally make their own selections and read at their own rate; the teacher works with individuals chiefly but also with groups or with the whole class on difficulties observed during individual sessions. Grouping, then, has real purpose.

Now we shall proceed to the actual operation of this approach. How did it start in the schools? What are the advantages? What are the problems? Our experience seems to be similar to the experiences reported elsewhere by others who have undertaken this approach.

Through our publications, informal reports, and personal contacts, some of the school personnel became aware of our point of view, and after further reading and inquiry decided to experiment in their own schools. The reading consultants of the Division of Elementary Schools who had had the opportunity to work with us on various projects helped in translating some of our ideas to the teachers and principals. They also assisted in setting up the program in some of the schools.

Two members of our Bureau staff are making a survey in the schools where Individualized Reading has been started. They are observing classes and interviewing principals, teachers, and pupils. I also have visited some of the schools. It is most stimulating to find such good thinking on the part of the school personnel and such excellent *implementation* of their thinking.

The principals preferred to go slowly at first, involving only those teachers who volunteered and were willing to experiment. The grades were mainly fourth and higher, although a number of primary classes were included.

Some of the preliminary steps taken were as follows:

> Getting as many suitable books into the classroom as possible; keeping books flowing in and out of classroom.
> Telling the children something about the changes in approach.
> Finding out the children's interests and personal feelings toward books and reading.

Determining the children's comfortable levels; their strengths and weaknesses; the specific skills needed.

Establishing necessary routines; developing self-management with respect to these routines.

Helping the child and the right book come together.

After visiting about 50 classes and making a survey of current practices, it was found that, although no two teachers worked exactly in the same way even in the same school, there emerged a general picture of their procedures:

Teachers generally gave some directions to the class as a whole.

A time was given when all children read independently from self-selected material.

Teachers held sessions or "conferences" with individual children or with a small group.

Teachers kept records of children's abilities, needs, and interests.

The children kept simple records and reports of their readings.

There was class or group discussion or sharing of books read.

The teachers devised various ways of working with the children. They might have the "conference" off in a corner of the room or they might walk down the aisles asking the children to read for them and giving aid when needed or asked for. They varied their procedures. They could not work with every child every day, nor was there sharing every day. The length of the sessions depended on the children, the size of the class, the material available, and the purposes of the children and the teacher. There was no precise pattern or set of rules which the teacher followed.

In the individualized reading approach, the teacher's role is crucial. She must plan carefully, budget her time, keep adequate records, evaluate her procedures, be flexible, resourceful, and creative. Incidentally, she should be that way in any program. The teachers observed were more aware and concerned about the skills than they had ever been in the basic reader program. They understood how to combine the skills instruction with the free-selection material. They also seemed to sense a better relationship between the amount of time given to skills development and the actual act of reading. This is the way one teacher expressed herself: "The mechanics are secondary. The teacher's understanding of how the mechanics are to be fitted in is important. It's the *meshing* of the mechanics and the actual reading that is inherent in Individualized Reading. At times the teacher actually cannot focus on the mechanics per se, if the reading is interfered with. However, with good planning she provides time for the development of mechanics."

In the discussion or "sharing" sessions, we observed more lively participation, interest, and attention on the part of the children than was ever possible in any other type of reading program. Wider vocabulary usage, deeper comprehension, and more critical thinking were evident. The activities described above were not limited to just certain "reading periods." Free-selection operated at other times, and skills were developed similarly in reading situations concerned with other curriculum areas.

The evaluation of this approach cannot be left to the use of standardized tests alone. Other observations are necessary in order to measure the *quality* and *depth* of the children's reading. What effect, for example, has reading on the child's thinking? What effect will it have on his life both now and later?

As in any program, some problems will arise. The teachers and principals expressed concern about:

*Materials*—there are not enough books as yet to fit the needs of the classes; administration and organization of the books are serious factors.

*Children's ability in selection*—some children may need special guidance that the teacher does not foresee.

*Teacher attitude*—fear of something new.

*Teacher effectiveness*—would all teachers be able to handle this approach?

*Supervision*—flexibility makes procedures more difficult to assess. If the supervisor understands and has the same objectives, evaluation will not be too difficult. He may, however, have to employ evaluative measures somewhat different in nature from the existing ones.

*Parents' reactions*—skepticism about changing procedures.

Observations have shown that the teachers and supervisors are meeting the challenge of these problems. The materials will always present difficulties. The public libraries are finding that even they do not have an adequate supply because of this new interest in reading.

The values of the individualized approach are too numerous to include in this paper. The most important will be summarized as follows:

*Values for the Child*

This approach:

Really provides for individual differences; satisfies children's needs of seeking, self-selection, and pacing.

Better integration with other language arts—more creative thinking and critical reading; wide increase in vocabulary; motivation for listening, writing, and spelling; strong desire to communicate ideas.

Decided carry-over to homes; more self-initiated reading; extensive use of public library.

Social interaction—good relationships within the class; acceptance of one another's contributions; "caste system" is broken down.

The child has a better sense of his own worth—self-understanding; he is a participating member of the group—he relies on his own self-management; he feels that he is a real part of the program and is learning from his own efforts and not always because of what the teacher wants him to learn.

Child actually reads; learns to cherish and handle books; respects authors and their ideas.

Observations and interviews with the children have indicated that they are happier, reading more, and learning more. Their testimonials are heart-warming. One boy remarked: "No matter what happens, I'm going to stick with it." Another boy wrote, "This is a healthier program." Upon being questioned to explain, he said, "Well, now I read all the books I like *in my class*. So now I don't have to read them after school, and I have time to play outside and that is healthier."

*Values and Rewarding Outcomes for the Teacher*

This approach leads to:

A one-to-one relationship with the child—it leads more closely to the child's needs—the teacher is a real helper.

The conclusion that interest, independence, and self-status of the children lessen the probability of behavior problems.

Increased teacher growth—there is greater responsibility on the part of the teacher in identifying and adjusting skills; in developing more long-term goals; in more thinking in terms of objectives and values.

Solving the problem of the wide range—it is more easily handled.

Integration of the curriculum—a natural outgrowth of this approach.

Increased status of teacher by participation in pioneer work— a real "grass roots" movement—she has opportunities to show her creativeness, resourcefulness, flexibility.

More support and active participation of supervisor.

Our observations and interviews have shown us that the teachers participating in the individualized approach are thoroughly satisfied and in most cases enthusiastic. I should like to close this paper with a quotation from an interview with a principal: "This is the best thing that has come along in the educational field for a long time. It seems so simple that one wonders why it wasn't hit upon before. This is truly getting at the individual. This is individualizing in fact and not in name only.

## "REPORTS OF ACTION RESEARCH"

*Lucy Polansky, Department of Education, Queens College, New York, and Ethel M. Schmidt, Jefferson School, Union, New Jersey*

*Dr. Polansky reports on the results of two third grade teachers who experimented with individualizing their reading program. Test results and observational data are included. Mrs. Schmidt reports on her own experiences in her own first grade class room, citing test results and other pertinent data.*

(By Lucy Polansky)

DURING THE FALL OF 1955, two teachers in a school affiliated with Queens College in an experimental program requested consultant help from the college in individualizing their reading program. The teachers had never seen such a program in action. During preliminary study they had formed the assumption that the use of individualized methods, with reading materials self-selected by the children, could be more valuable to their children than the three-group method of basal reader instruction which the teachers were then using. But they feared that the children might suffer loss in reading growth while their teachers attempted to learn ways of teaching which were very different from the method in general use in their school.

From *Reading In Action,* 1957, Proceedings of the International Reading Association Conference in New York City. Reprinted by permission of the author and the International Reading Association.

Through a cooperative research project, the teachers were able to develop their own ways of working, at their own pace. Instead of receiving training in the use of a method, the teachers were to develop methodology as they selected, adapted, created and refined procedures consonant with their understanding of their children's needs and interests. It was believed that other teachers in the school might receive some stimulation and guidance from this project if findings could be recorded and shared. The success of the programs developed by the two teachers was to be evaluated in terms of the progress of the children involved and the job satisfaction of their teachers.

Both teachers taught third-grade children of average intelligence; both had been considered successful teachers of reading; both were probationary teachers in New York City.

From January until June, 1956, the teachers met for an hour's conference each week with the consultant, graduate student assistant and other teachers. Continuous study of the children in each classroom provided a basis for group discussion and problem solving.

The teachers did not wish to discard their basal reader programs entirely until they had found partial solutions to the major problems they encountered. But by April, three months after the teachers' efforts had been formalized into a cooperative research project, each teacher had developed an apparently successful, fully individualized reading program.

Data were supplied through before-and-after tests utilizing different forms of two standardized reading tests, through anecdotal records based on group and individual observations by the graduate student assistant, through a sociometric questionnaire, through record cards kept by the teacher to indicate each child's daily progress and specific needs, and through teacher observations and interpretations.

According to median scores achieved on the Metropolitan

Reading Tests, Forms S and T, the gain for each group between January and April was six months' reading achievement.
According to the results of the regular school testing program,
the reading growth recorded for the year was again the same
for both groups—one year and two months. The Gilmore Oral
Reading Tests, Forms A and B, administered in February and
May, indicated gains analogous to those shown by the Metropolitan Test. The Gilmore tests were valuable in helping the
teachers diagnose the children's reading difficulties and in providing a code for recording on cards the difficulties the children
encountered during daily experiences.

Analysis of data from other sources became more important
to the teachers than the standardized test scores, as their research proceeded. The major growths in the children which
the teachers' analyses revealed were in the main those which
have already been reported in similar studies. The teachers
were nevertheless impressed by the new joy in reading which
the children showed, by the children's deeper appreciation of
poetry and their increasing discrimination in selection of reading materials, by their rapidly growing independence and self-
direction, and by their ability to hold audience interest when
reading orally.

When the year ended, the research group organized its findings and wrote a report which could be duplicated and circulated to the school staff during the next school year.

In a school system in which there is growing interest in individualized reading, it is difficult to estimate the influence of the
work of two teachers on one school. However, it is true that
there has been a definite trend toward individualization in this
school. The most significant single change was perhaps that
shown in the results of a questionnaire circulated to all teachers
by the school principal in 1957. When indicating the kinds of
consultant help desired, 23 of a staff of 42 teachers asked for

help in individualizing their reading programs or in planning some cooperative study for the improvement of individualization they had already begun. A series of workshops has since been initiated. Full attendance (voluntary) and high interest have been consistent.

It seems that supervisors and teachers who wish to help their colleagues achieve desired curriculum changes may find that action research pays dividends in terms of long-range effects.

### (By Ethel M. Schmidt)

When first-grade students came to me in September, I usually followed a certain procedure. After a period of getting acquainted and observation I would identify those children in need of further readiness work and those who seemed ready to begin reading instruction. Later the class was divided into three or four groups—each group of children at about the same stage of readiness and with roughly the same rates of learning. Then reading instructions would proceed in the generally accepted way.

However, I was not quite satisfied that this situation would measure up when judged in the light of achieving the best possible climate for developing good mental health. It seemed to me that children too readily identified themselves and their friends as being members of the best or the slowest reading group, and that they transferred this feeling of achievement or lack of achievement in reading to other aspects of school life.

This led me to attempt individual instruction in reading at the first-grade level.

I discussed my plans with the school principal. She not only approved but offered to co-operate wherever possible.

The 25 children (19 Negro and 7 white) who entered my class the following September were from families of middle and low socio-economic levels. They soon found many opportunities for expressing their ideas and emotions through art forms, music and rhythms. They listened to stories, played games and went for walks—the usual reading-readiness activities. Here I changed my routine—no groups were formed for formal reading.

There were several copies each of many pre-primers on the library shelves and, before long, the children discovered that if they selected a book and brought it to me during free time they could show me the pictures and talk about them. Of course the next step was, "What does that say?" Then came, "I know what that says. I remember." Then reading instruction had begun for that child.

The success of this plan, it seems to me, rests largely with the type of records kept. Individual pupil cards were kept on which I jotted down a kind of anecdotal record of each child. The books that he chose and the pages that he read were noted. As he progressed into the primer stage, special difficulties were noted and special help was provided for him.

Soon everyone was eager to participate. Often a child would gather several friends together and read to them. Here was a real audience situation, and the reader had to measure up to group standards. It seemed to me that reading had become an interesting thing to do in itself.

During this initial period the Department of Psychological Testing saw that each child was given a Stanford Binet test. When this was completed, we found that the group make-up was as follows:

*Chronological ages:* 5 years 6 months to 6 years 9 months.

*Intelligence quotients:* 87 to 121—1 below 90, 13 from 90 to 100, 6 from 100 to 110, and 5 above 110.

Mental age: 6 to 8 years—15 children had mental ages of

less than 6 years and 6 months as of the beginning of first grade.

As more and more children wanted individual help in reading, it was necessary to augment the 45-minute "free time" of the morning. We added 35 minutes for reading in the afternoon. As the children grew in maturity, this afternoon time was devoted to completing assignments in number work and writing or reading to follow directions. The schedule was kept flexible.

As the children grew in reading ability, more difficult books were put on the shelves. Children were still free to select their own material. No child was required to start at the beginning of a book and read to the end. There was no word drill by groups of children, and no workbooks were used.

At the close of first grade, the children were given the Gates Primary Tests. The results showed an average reading grade placement from 1.5 to 2.54. Ten children were above the norm, one at the norm, and 15 fell below. The median reading grade was 1.8. Eighteen children averaged a higher reading age than mental age, and 7 averaged a lower reading age than mental age.

It was decided that I would continue this same program with the same group of children for another year. In Grade 2, reading instruction was the same and spelling instruction was introduced. Children suggested words that they would like to learn to spell and several of those most frequently chosen were studied by the entire class each week.

At the close of second grade, Gates Primary Reading Tests and Gates Advanced Primary Reading Tests were administered. Two of the children who ranked lowest in the Primary Tests did not take the Advanced Primary Tests. The Primary Test results showed that 14 children scored above the norm and 11 below. Advanced Primary Test results showed 9 children above the norm, 3 at the norm and 11 below. The final scores on the Primary Tests ranged from 1.53 to 3.44 and on the Advanced Primary 1.8 to 4.1.

All records for each child were sent on to the next teacher.

At present I am carrying on the following type of action research. I have selected four children from my second-grade class of 31. These four were selected because they are most seriously retarded in reading. I am attempting to use the techniques usually used in remedial reading clinics to help these children. I have made an individual study and tentative diagnosis for each child and am recording all work done with them. They were given the Gates Primary Reading Tests at the start of this work and will be given another form of the same test at the end of May. This, combined with informal tests, will enable me to judge whether or not this procedure seems valuable enough to repeat with other classes.

# INDIVIDUALIZED READING
# IN ACTION

*Elizabeth Young, Fifth Grade Teacher,*
*Baltimore Public Schools*
*Karel Newman, Fourth Grade Teacher,*
*New York City Public Schools*

*Mrs. Young describes how her classroom operates during her reading period. She tells how her children help find enough books, how the independent activities are set up, and what goes on during the personal individual reading conferences. Miss Newman tells how she proceeded in her fourth grade to set up an individualized reading program. There is a particularly good description of the sharing or "pooling" period, when children tell each other about the books they have read.*

## (By Elizabeth Young)

I WAS ASKED to describe for you our way of learning to read in my fifth grade. There is nothing I would rather talk about.

I have been doing individualized reading since my third year of teaching. In the five years that have passed, I have learned a lot about it. My children learn to read from books they choose. I do not find it necessary to "motivate" them to read. Reading books that they have chosen is as natural to them as breathing.

From *Reading In Action,* 1957, Proceedings of the International Reading Association Conference in New York City. Reprinted by permission of the author and the International Reading Association.

We have no groups labeled according to ability. There is no need for children of higher reading ability to feel superior, or children of lower ability to want to pull Joan's hair because she can read anything she picks up. The minimum achievement gain for any child has been 12 months.

My children are so fascinated with the idea of choosing their own books that they explore every possible source to get them. They comb all of the libraries they can find. The Enoch Pratt Free Library started us off this year with a box of 45 books—one for each child. In addition, each child brought in two or three books on his own. Our supply is around 125-150 books for my 45 children.

### Starting the Reading Period

Often my children like to come in before the bell rings. Any morning you might find several children reading leisurely from humorous books (before the serious business of the day begins!), another at the easel painting on a story illustration, or a twosome in a corner reading parts of a book to each other. And it is truly upsetting to have the bell interrupt such activity in order to "begin school."

But begin it we must, and after the usual opening ceremonies, I start out by holding up from five to ten books which I have found. I am always sure of "takers." This is what happens when children choose their own reading books.

Next we plan together the various activities—after their silent reading—that are to be carried on while I have my individual or group reading conferences. Each child has in mind some idea, and if he doesn't (which is not often) I am ready with suggestions.

Once I am sure that things will be peaceful, quiet and busy, we are ready to begin the reading conferences. The children take turns coming to me to read from their self-selected pieces of material. During these individual sessions I notice their reading weaknesses. They might lack skill in attacking words, in thinking critically, in making inferences, or in getting a central thought. As each child comes to me, I take notes about his reading and the kind of skill he needs practice in most. I check his reading, or test his ability to get meaning from books.

Each child in the class has a page in my notebook for entries concerning his reading progress. Other data on the page might be his latest reading test result, his IQ, as well as the books from which he has read to me.

From these records I can get a running picture of a child's reading since we have been together. But also I am able to plan the best way to save time by grouping those who have similar needs, and helping them all at the same time.

### The Use of Experiences in Reading

I find in my class, as many teachers do with enrollments of 40 to 47, children who need special work on vocabulary building. Several of my children are far below the grade reading level. They need much help. I have just the cure for that. We make a co-operative reader together. We call it "Class Diary." It is simply a story of all of the wonderful and exciting things that happen to us from day to day. They like to read from their Diary which we always keep available. I find these slow readers have much less trouble when they are reading something that is a part of them.

Other reading activities can be developed from our Diary. A second day after a given experience, we can work on compound words, for example: "sawdust." Or we might study prefixes or suffixes as in the words "unexpected" and "comfortably."

Among my favorite groups are those that form from pure

interest—we call them "reporters." They read books on different topics of interest to the class and then report facts at the end of the period. For example, one day they might read and report on dogs. On another day it might be weather. And so it goes.

We finish our reading period by sharing all that we feel is of interest to the class—reports, dramatizations, demonstrations in the area of science, or plugs for books that someone has liked particularly well. Through these sharings I have wonderful opportunities to plan for the next day. We don't have any dull moments in my fifth-grade class because we are simply too busy—working, sharing and living.

### (By Karel Newman)

The individualized reading program has operated in my classroom for the past two years. When I volunteered to institute it in my classroom, I had a fourth-grade group, average and above average in reading ability. My principal was most enthusiastic about the program and sent me many new trade books. The very fact that we were not using the standard basal readers and were able to choose from a variety of authors and kinds of books created an enchantment for both the students and teacher.

In organizing the mechanics of the program, my primary objective was to instill as strong a motivation to read as possible. I placed the most attractive books and jackets in accessible places in the room. Signs such as, "Scientists Sit Here," "Have You Read These?" and "Who Is Horton?" were prominently displayed. For the first week, the children were not permitted to read the books. I created story hours by candlelight, talked about the books, showed pictures, read blurbs, excerpts and first chapters from about 25 books that covered a variety of categories. Particularly effective for this type of treatment were *The Hundred Dresses* [1] and *Mr. Popper's Penguins*.[2] This year I had the added advantage of being able to call upon children from last year to tell the class about their experiences with certain books and authors. We thought of books in categories fulfilling certain interest requirements.

After the class's interest seemed considerably heightened and I felt reasonably sure that each child would try to find a book, I explained the program. Each child was to choose his book and read it only as long as it held his interest.

My next task was to test the children. There had been Standardized Reading Tests given at the end of the third year. Now I used the Informal Book Test which gave specific instructions for discovering reading deficiencies. This helped me to understand where specific problems lay. I was to continue discovering difficulties by means of the many individual interviews which followed.

By this point in the term, the reading period extends for one hour. Frequently, the first ten minutes are devoted to the teaching of a skill that is needed by the entire class. At this time, there may also follow a short explanation of the purpose of what we call the "pooling period" for the day so that the children may be clear on what is expected of them.

The actual reading period is approximately 40 minutes. The children select their books and settle down to read. While they are reading, I may assist in one of several ways. A group that shares a common skill difficulty may meet with me to work and drill on the problem. We use pages from workbooks that are applicable to the specific skill area. If I am not working with a group, during the course of the period, I may interview four or five children intensively and thus continue to discover

---

[1] Eleanor Estes, *The Hundred Dresses*. New York: Harcourt Brace, 1944.
[2] Richard and Florence Atwater, *Mr. Popper's Penguins*. Boston: Little, Brown, 1938.

specific weaknesses and provide drill work. In the case of the more advanced reader, I may be working on only comprehension and contextual problems. A more general overview of the class work may be gleaned if I walk around and sit with twelve or fifteen children during the hour. During the reading time, I may be called upon to answer questions about individual reading problems or help in the selection of books.

The "pooling period" is the climax of the hour; this sharing of books may be directed within broad categories. Some provocative questions are asked about characters and situations in books that have been read. The children, depending upon their particular abilities, will answer these questions on face value or read into the problem their own meanings. We might even pool with kinds of words or phrases, sensory, action or descriptive. This unifying of the class at the beginning and end of the period makes for a healthy classroom atmosphere that discourages the competitive aspects of group work.

No really effective reading program can be restricted to a specified time limit. The children will see that it naturally spills over into other curriculum areas. The children are enthusiastic about their reading and wish to express their feelings in positive responses. Language arts is a fertile field. Using books of cartoons that we have read, the children have made up their own captions. Innumerable plays and playlets have been acted, and some written. Poetry has been more and more appreciated since we have read so much and so many different kinds. Every child in my class has written at least two original stories, not necessarily fiction, but covering poetry, autobiography, science, mystery, etc. The children have improved their writing technique to encourage answers from authors, many of whom have responded personally, which has heightened interest considerably.

More important than my reaction is the spontaneous feeling

that the children have about the program. They love it and their work is a reflection of this attitude. I heard comments like these: "It's like finding freedom," "You owe me 15 minutes of reading," "You can read without rushing," "What happens if I have to have a reader next term?," "You feel grownup," "We learn more this way." In case we think that we have fooled them with our grouping, one or two have been known to say, "I like this way of reading; there are no slow or fast groups."

Based on my experience with the program, the most salient aspects are the inbreeding of this great desire to read. Each child in my class has read approximately 25 books at this point of the term. Here is a program that in actual practice has developed a love and respect for reading in almost every child exposed to it and at the same time has stressed skills teaching based on individual needs and differences.

# TEACHING READING THE INDIVIDUALIZED WAY

*Helen K. Mackintosh, Chief of Elementary School Section, U. S. Office of Education*
*Mary Helen Mahar, Children's Library Specialist, U. S. Office of Education*

> *Dr. Mackintosh and Miss Mahar here attempt to clarify a point of difference among educators—the need for a controlled vocabulary. In addition, the article is particularly helpful to teachers embarking on the use of trade books.*

ONLY THE PERSON who knows from experience the pleasures and uses of reading can even imagine the problems facing a child who cannot read well. The understanding teacher of any group of children recognizes their wide differences in reading ability and works to help each child succeed in terms of his capacity. Her methods are useful tools; to be certain they are right for her purpose, she turns upon them the hard light of one question after another:

*Do I have valid reasons for selecting one method of organizing teaching-learning experiences and for rejecting another? Do I put the stamp of "good" on certain ways of working just because they have been used for a long time, and "poor" on ways relatively new although there is some evidence that they give good results? Do I supplement what I have learned*

Courtesy of *School Life,* May, 1958.

*from my training and experience with knowledge that has come out of recent research?*

For this teacher in today's school, are there any principles to guide her in her choice of practices?

### An Individual Matter

Some of the statements about reading that are appearing in professional magazines provide one basis for evaluating practices. For example, these:

We still fail to teach about 15 percent of our pupils to read successfully.—*Spache*

By the time a class has entered the sixth grade, the range in reading abilities may be from zero to about the 12th grade.—*Betts*

There is a widespread acceptance of the importance of individualized reading instruction.—*Shane*

Reading is a highly individual matter, and each child differs from every other child in ability to read. Educators should pay more attention to this fact in evaluating methods of teaching and learning. The skill of recognizing words and getting thought from the printed page is basic in the reading process, but the more complex skills of using the thought for some purpose is of even greater importance. People read, for example, to get help in solving a problem, to give themselves pleasure, or to have something to share with others. Such purposes must be accepted by the child as his own. As the writer of a recent magazine article said, "If children like books, they'll read."

Although children's reading interests can be identified for any age level—preschool, primary, or intermediate—and reading materials selected to suit them, there are many reading materials with qualities that appeal to readers of all ages—qualities such as good story, action, adventure, and humor. For children who are just beginning to read and for children who have difficulty with reading, it is highly important to use materials rich in these qualities. The teacher will be wise to remember also that most children have personal interests that can be used to attract them to books. Not all children are gifted academically, but every child has gifts the teacher can find and use as "handles" to bring him and his book together. Three things about the child—his interest, ability, and background— should be part of any consideration of teaching and learning as it relates to reading.

As Dr. Betts points out, children in any grade are at widely different stages of reading ability. But in their attitudes toward reading, favorable or unfavorable, nursery and kindergarten children, as well as older girls and boys, reflect their parents. Parents are helpful when they show interest in books and use every means to extend and enrich children's experiences and vocabularies; but when they put pressure on children to make them learn to read, they probably defeat their own purposes.

## Teaching Methods

The preceding discussion is preamble to a look at currently accepted methods of teaching reading. There are no figures to cite, but many teachers in the United States are probably still attempting to teach reading from a single text, requiring every child in the class to read the same page in the same book at the same time. Busy teachers, new teachers, teachers with large classes—all these and others have often accepted the practice, for a variety of reasons.

Probably the most widely used method of teaching reading in 1958 is based on some form of grouping. Grouping means many things to many people, but a generally accepted meaning is the dividing of a class into three groups, usually on the basis of ability. A teacher using this plan should realize what such grouping does to children. A child in the "best" group may be self-satisfied, may brag a bit, may refer condescendingly to those who do not read well. A child in the middle group may be satisfied to be average, since most people in the world *are* that. But the child in the "poor" group has little incentive, for no matter how much he improves, he still will probably remain in that group.

Dr. Dolch suggests that a teacher who wants to understand the effects of grouping on children should try to imagine herself in similar circumstances. Suppose the superintendent of schools divided his faculty into three groups on the basis of ability. How would the teacher in the lowest group feel? Would she do better work? Or poorer?

There are classes where children are divided into two groups rather than three. Others are divided into five or more: this is the kind of grouping Dr. Dolch says teachers would need if they "honestly" followed the reading levels of children. There are a number of written reports describing how a teacher has worked with five or more groups in her classroom. In these situations, however, groups are organized on a basis that keeps them flexible rather than fixed—not on the basis of ability but on the basis of a sociometric study, a purpose, a problem, or a specific need.

## Individualized Reading

Among the teachers who think of reading as a highly individual process, an ever-increasing number with creative imagination are developing plans for children's reading experiences that are variously called individualized, self-selected, self-pacing, personalized, or reading by invitation. Some teachers move into an individualized program from a situation in which they have 3, 5, 6, or 7 groups. Others individualize instruction from the start. How each one proceeds depends upon (1) her own ability to organize, (2) her ability to work with children, (3) the size of her group, (4) the previous experience of her pupils, (5) her knowledge about books of different degrees of difficulty and different interest appeals, and (6) the availability of such books.

In the new publication edited by Alice Miel, several teachers tell how they got under way in individualized programs of reading. Some teachers were fortunate enough to have small classes; others began with a group within the class; and one, beginning with seven groups, used them as springboards to seven individualized programs in which children helped each other get started. Success seems to depend not so much on how the teacher gets started or whether she uses many different books either alone or in combination with textbooks, as on her own interest and the interest of the children.

One of the problems of the teacher who uses several individual books, or "trade" books, is that they do not provide her with the controlled vocabulary that is one of the most important features of a textbook series. *It is on this issue—whether a controlled vocabulary is essential—that educators disagree.*\* But if repetition is desired, the teacher can use a book like Wanda Gag's *Millions of Cats,* which has a great deal of repetition but provides it in the framework of a story that has action, good story, adventure, and humor.

Although trade books are primarily the starting point for the teacher in an individualized reading program, this fact does not preclude the use of textbooks once the child understands that he is reading and progressing as an individual, not as a member of a group, and is following his own progress through his own record, kept in either graphic or anecdotal form.

It is certain that more research is needed to evaluate individualized and group procedures in the teaching of reading. Surely researchers need to scrutinize present methods of teach-

\* Editor's italics.

ing beginning reading, rather than to concentrate solely on the remedial programs for those who have not succeeded in learning to read. After reviewing findings of studies published over a 50-year period, Dr. Gray concludes that there is a place for both the group and the individualized methods of teaching reading.

## Value of the School Library

Teaching reading by the individualized method requires plentiful resources of children's books. An elementary school library with an organized collection of children's books and other material, administered by a professional librarian and open at all times of the schoolday to teachers and children, is essential to a fully developed reading program in the elementary school. From it, with the assistance of the librarian, teachers can select classroom collections which they can continually refresh by making new selections.

A centralized elementary school library makes the whole collection of children's books available to every grade and classroom: the same books can be used at different times by every grade in the school and thus meet the need of every child. For example, in a third-grade room some children read at the first-grade level; others at the second; still others at the third-, fourth-, fifth-, and sixth-grade levels; and many children read at different levels at different times. In the reading program planned to serve these highly individual needs, the elementary school library not only provides a valuable service, but provides it economically.

In elementary schools not yet equipped with school libraries, principals and teachers interested in teaching reading by the individualized method should develop classroom collections, following as closely as possible the basic principles of the centralized school library. These collections should be selected from recognized lists of children's books, and should be interchanged at intervals among classrooms. Among the materials that teachers will find helpful in organizing these collections and developing activities related to reading are Jacobs' leaflet, and others, in a bulletin entitled *Adventuring in Literature with Children.*

Books should be displayed on shelves and tables in every classroom so as to stimulate children's reading interests in an atmosphere conducive to the enjoyment of books. If these displays are changed from time to time, they will make an intriguing kaleidoscope of different types of reading material; sometimes they can be used to present stories, folktales, or poetry; other times, realistic books about airplanes and trucks or home and community life; other times, factual books related to units of study in the curriculum—social studies, science, and mathematics. There are children's trade books on all these subjects, and they can be used to teach not only reading but every other subject in the curriculum. In this manner, learning through reading becomes a rich experience, and reading itself becomes a natural and joyful activity for boys and girls.

## Lists and Criteria

Teachers accustomed to using graded textbooks for teaching reading may sometimes have difficulty in selecting trade books for the individualized method. Children's trade books, however, are graded in a broad sense—for instance, as appealing to the youngest readers, from 3 to 5 years old, or to children from 10 to 12. In addition, most standard and recognized lists of children's trade books indicate the age level or grade range for each book listed. *Children's Catalog* lists and notes the grade range for 3,204 books; *A Basic Book Collection for Elementary Grades* does the same for more than 1,000 books.

Both *Adventuring with Books,* a list for the elementary grades, and *Bibliography of Books for Children* indicate age range.

These lists, all compiled by experienced teachers and librarians from the whole field of children's literature, are highly useful guides. Not only are they frequently revised and brought up to date but they are annotated and arranged by subject or interest category. In *Bibliography of Books for Children,* for example, such subject headings as "Picture Storybooks," "Animals of All Kinds," "Holidays To Celebrate," and "Fanciful Stories and Folklore Collections," lead the teacher to many attractive and interesting books for children aged 4 to 12; others, like "Earth Studies" and "Experiments To Try" and "Music" point out books varied in approach and level of difficulty to suit the needs of elementary children of all grades. A companion list, *Children's Books for $1.25 or Less,* useful in choosing inexpensive books for a new elementary school collection, also is subdivided by subject. Teachers unfamiliar with children's books can depend on such lists in beginning a collection and can acquire knowledge of the books as they use them.

Several authoritative periodicals also annotate and grade new books for children. Among them are the *Horn Book,* the *Booklist* and *Subscription Books Bulletin,* the *Bulletin of the Children's Book Center,* and the magazine, *Elementary English.*

The American Library Association publishes a comprehensive catalog of tools for book selection, giving the source and price of each. It can be purchased in quantity, but single copies are available free on request. The aids it lists should be available in every school library.

Some teachers may want to augment their knowledge of children's books and to improve their understanding of criteria for selecting them. They may wish to become less dependent on lists, and to develop their own ability to evaluate critically in terms of the special interests of all the children in their classrooms. There are many fine books about children's literature that discuss criteria for selecting different types of children's books. Two should be especially helpful, one by Arbuthnot and one by Smith.

## The Child's Choice

Children who are being taught to read by the individualized method should be encouraged to select freely, both in the library and in the classroom, books they like. Usually a child will naturally select a book he can read, or a book so close to his interest that he will increase his skill as he reads it. Children generally reject books that are too hard, too easy, or lacking in appeal.

Sometimes a child needs to be told something about the books that will encourage his selection or give him confidence to take a book to read, but he should not be discouraged from browsing and experimenting. There are many intangibles working in a child's selection of a book—color, size, illustrations, relation of the story to his experience, his own personality—and if, in giving guidance, the teacher permits these intangibles to have free play, the child will probably select the book that is right for him. In contrast, if his teacher selects a book for him and assigns it as a class exercise, he is not so likely to gain anything from it. He may master the words through repetition and drill, but the experience may—and often does—destroy his interest in further reading.

### Pleasure Is Basic

The individualized method of teaching reading does not preclude all the shared group and class experiences that children can have with books and reading. They love storytelling; and storytelling by the teacher, the librarian, and sometimes by the children should be part of the reading program. Sometimes this storytelling can take place in the library or outdoors under a tree. It may be a good procedure at times to divide children into groups so that they can tell each other the stories they have read. The school librarian may bring new books to the classroom and talk about them, or the teacher may want to tell the class about some of the new books. Children enjoy choral speaking of poetry, which gives them an opportunity for creative self-expression. All experiences of the individualized reading program—children selecting their own books, reading quietly as individuals, reading to each other, listening to a story, or speaking poetry—should be considered basic to the teaching of reading, and not treated as "free period" activities, or as rewards for reading an assigned book or "finishing" sooner than the time assigned.

Children's out-of-school and home experiences with reading should be considered as part of the whole reading program. Teachers and school librarians will find that cooperation with public librarians in introducing children to the public library will encourage children to use the children's room of the public library after school and on Saturdays. Children's specialists on public library staffs can often come to the school and talk about books or plan book fairs and exhibits with the teachers and school librarians. Useful guides can be made available to parents interested in buying books for the child's home library —lists like one prepared by Arbuthnot, for example.

Every child needs a place at home for his own books. A child's ownership of books with a special corner or shelf for them helps to develop in him an affection for books and a sense of security that is an essential part of growing up.

Children's attitudes toward reading will profoundly affect their reading ability. If children, in learning to read, also learn to *like* to read, their approach to all schoolwork involving reading will be more favorable to learning and understanding. The individualized method of teaching reading has implications for pupil achievement that are immeasurable. The growth of individuals in our democracy is in large measure dependent upon their ability to read with intelligence, discrimination, and enjoyment.

## BIBLIOGRAPHY

American Library Association, *Aids in Selection of Materials for Children and Young People: Books, Films, Records,* Chicago, 1957.

———— *A Basic Book Collection for Elementary Grades,* Miriam Snow, Mather, chairman, Chicago, 1956.

———— *Booklist and Subscription Books Bulletin,* Chicago.

Arbuthnot, May Hill, *Children and Books,* rev. ed., New York, 1957.

———— *Children's Books Too Good to Miss,* Cleveland, 1953.

Association for Childhood Education International, *Bibliography of Books for Children,* Christine B. Gilbert, chairman, Washington, 1956 ed.

———— *Children's Books for $1.25 or Less,* Sybil Ann Hanna, comp., and Alida H. Hisle, staff ed., Washington, 1957.

Betts, Emmet Albert, "Reading and the Fourth R," *Elementary English,* vol. 35, No. 1, January 1958.

*Bulletin of the Children's Book Center,* University of Chicago Press, Chicago.

Dolch, E. W., "Groups in Reading," *Elementary English,* vol. 34, No. 6, October 1957.

Gag, Wanda, *Millions of Cats,* New York, 1928.

Gray, William S., "Role of Group and Individualized Teaching in a Sound Reading Program," *The Reading Teacher,* vol. 11, December, 1957.

*Horn Book Magazine,* Horn Book Inc., Boston.

Jacobs, Leland B., "Building a Balanced Classroom Library," leaflet in Bulletin 92, *Adventuring in Literature with Children,* Constance Carr, ed., Association for Childhood Education International, Washington, 1953.

Kingsley, Marjorie, "An Experiment in Individualized Reading," *Elementary English,* February, 1958, pp. 113-118.

McConnell, Marion L., and West, Dorothy Herbert, *Children's Catalog,* 9th ed., New York, 1956.

Miel, Alice, ed., *Individualizing Reading Practices,* Practical Suggestions for Teaching, No. 14, Teachers College, Columbia University, New York, 1958.

National Council of Teachers of English, *Adventuring with Books,* Mabel F. Alstetter, chairman, Champaign, Ill., 1956.

―――― *Elementary English,* Champaign, Ill. Shane, Harold G., "The First R," *Research Helps in Teaching the Language Arts,* Association for Supervision and Curriculum Development, Washington, 1955.

Smith, Lillian H., *The Unreluctant Years: A Critical Approach to Children's Literature,* American Library Association, Chicago, Ill., 1953.

Spache, George D., "New Approaches to Research in Language Arts," *Elementary English,* vol. 34, No. 6, October 1957.

# Appendix

## SAMPLE OF TEACHERS' RECORDS

| Name | | Test Score | | |
|------|------|------|------|------|
| Age | | I.Q. | | |
| Date | Book | Interests | Skills Needed | Group or Individual Assignments |
| | | | | |
| | | | | |

| Name | | Reading Score | | |
|------|------|------|------|------|
| Age | | I.Q. | | |
| Date | Book | Comments | Special Work Needed | Good Points. Today's Reading |
| | | | | |
| | | | | |

## SAMPLE OF TEACHERS' RECORDS

| Name | | |
| --- | --- | --- |
| Book and Date | Related Independent Work | Optional Independent Work |
| | | |

| GROUP WORK | | | | |
| --- | --- | --- | --- | --- |
| Date | Content Covered | Children Assigned | Future Work on 1. Content | 2. Children |
| | | | | |

## Sample: Profile Chart

| Name   *Ronnie D.* | Book<br>"Angus & the cat"<br>Date   10-24 | Book<br>Date | Book<br>Date |
|---|---|---|---|
| Oral | | | |
| 1.  Word by word Reading | ✓ | | |
| 2.  Pointing | | | |
| 3.  Limited Sight vocabulary | ✓ VERY | | |
| a.  Lack of context clues | ✓ | | |
| b.  Lack of phonic skills | ✓ | | |
| c.  Endings | ✓ | | |
| 4.  Substitutions | ✓ | | |
| 5.  Repetitions | | | |
| 6.  Omissions | ✓ | | |
| 7.  Reversals | ✓ | | |
| 8.  Insertions | | | |
| 9.  Speed | | | |
| 10. Poor expression | ✓ | | |
| 11. Poor enunciation | | | |
| 12. Actual speech defect | | | |
| 13. Comprehension | | | |
| 14. Hesitation | ✓ | | |
| 15. Volume too loud | | | |
| 16. Volume too soft | | | |
| 17. Phrasing | ✓ | | |
| | | | |
| Silent | | | |
| 1.  Habits | | | |
| a.  Pointing | | | |
| b.  Vocalizations | | | |
| c.  Speed | | | |
| d.  Short attention span | ✓ | | |
| 2.  Lack of comprehension | | | |
| a.  Getting the main idea | | | |
| b.  Noting details | | | |
| 1) stated | | | |
| 2) implied | | | |
| c.  Understanding concepts | | | |
| d.  Making inferences | | | |
| e.  Following directions | | | |
| 3.  Lack of word study skills | | | |
| a.  Using book aids (Index, etc.) | | | |
| b.  Using reference material | | | |
| 1) locating information | | | |
| 2) skimming | | | |
| 3) organizing facts | | | |
| c.  Using dictionary aids | | | |
| d.  Using graphic aids | | | |

Used by Marilyn Zucker, 4th grade, Farmingdale Schools, New York.
Can be duplicated.

## Excerpts from First Grade
## Running Log of Mrs. Mary Bulcken
## Baltimore Public Schools

| Date | Name—Carl T. |
|------|------|
| 12/1 | "Under the Sky" |
| (12/3)[1] | Assign: Carl suggested a picture of Alice, Jerry, the pond and some squirrels |
| 12/7 | With, on, little my (ed. missed words) |
| | "We Look and See" (home) Fine! |
| | "We Work and Play" (home) |
| 12/9 | Assign:—Draw a ring around little words |
| | —example, boats - a u s endings |
| 12/15 | Assign: Illustrate |
| | Three big *cookies* |
| | Here is my *yellow* car |
| | Here we go in the big *blue* boat |
| | I see something in the sea |
| | "Guess Who"      J/Primer |
| | Not long after Carl had his new book he said, "My book has 95 pages and I have already read 23 of them." |
| 12/16 | When Carl came in this morning, he read his book, came to me and said "May I read a story to the class?" He did! Splendidly. |
| (12/21)[1] | "New Fun With Dick and Jane" |
| | Carl read one group of stories. We decided to do this because the book is so long. Carl is eager to |
| 1/12 [1] | read to family. |
| 1/18 · | library *very* pleased |
| (1/21)[1] | |
| 1/26 | Fine—"At the Farm" |
| (2/2[1], 2/4[1]) | Carl always has an extra book ready (ed. to read to teacher). He likes to have something to take home. |
| 2/16 | Carl read a story for opening exercises (fine) he also selected "My Little Green Story Book" |
| | I asked him why he chose it—he said "because I haven't read it yet—and I love to read." I *must* find more challenging material for him. |
| | |
| Date | Name—Joel G. |
| Mar. 8 | School and Play (difficult) |
| | Peter's Family |
| | Needed "is" "wants" |
| Mar. 10 | Read one story well. "I've been working and I like it, too." |

[1] Dates child also read—comments omitted to save space.

| | |
|---|---|
| **Mar. 21** | Bingo Gets the Boys Out<br>Attitude good. Tells Mother he can read best in<br>the class. |
| **Mar. 29** | Joel read one story hesitantly—<br>needed a lot of words—I thought perhaps it was too<br>difficult. |
| **Apr.** | Joel has found material he *can* read—<br>knew *every* word of "The Boy Who Went to the North Wind." |
| **June 1** | "I have a story all picked out! Ready?"<br>I was writing here when Joel said "Ready?" |

| | |
|---|---|
| **Date** | *Name—Bruce B.* |
| **May 31** | Bruce said "I have a story *all* ready!<br>*You* will love it!" |

| | |
|---|---|
| **Date** | *Name—Billy T.* |
| **Jan. 4** | Billy is satisfied with *one* story |
| **Jan. 10** | Read *one* story smoothly and knew all words |
| **Jan. 14, 19,<br>24 about** | |
| **2/2** | Billy read *one* story again, and then stood up.<br>I said "Billy wouldn't you like to read another?" He<br>said "NO." |
| **2/2** | Read fairly well, knew all vocabulary and talked about<br>the story.<br>Vocabulary check excellent. |
| **2/7** | Satisfied with *one* story<br>I do *not* insist.<br>"Up and Down" |
| **2/18** | After each story Billy looked up as though he wanted<br>to stop. I smiled and said, "Go ahead—you are<br>surprising yourself, aren't you? He laughed and<br>said "Yes."<br>Expression good! "My Little Green Story Book"<br>"Skip Along"<br>"Bing" |

## SAMPLE OF CHILDREN'S RECORDS

| Name | | | |
|------|------|------|------|
| Book Title | Author | Dates | Opinion of Book |
| | | | |

(3 x 5 card, one for each book)

Name
Book
Dates
Comments
Recommendation

| Name | | |
|------|------|------|
| Book and Author | Dates | Sharing Activity |
| | | |

## Teacher Records (excerpted)[1]

### Name John A.

| Book and Date | Briefing of Plot | Attitude | Word Recognition[2] | Skills Needed |
|---|---|---|---|---|
| 12/11 More Streets and Roads | OK | | and looked/to look starting/staring (self corrected) shout/shouted Miss/Mrs. | 12/2 Endings |
| 12/15 How the Grinch Stole Christmas | OK Got moral and offered it. | Needs much pushing, but some improvement. | But/by (self correction) snows/snooze trippings/trappings | Punctuation Good word attack on new words, but no attention to basic words |

### Name Jean D.

| Book and Date | Briefing of Plot | Attitude | Word Recognition | Skills Needed |
|---|---|---|---|---|
| 2/3 Surprise Island | OK | Needed help to find book | took hold | vowels, comprehension |

### Name Bobby

| Book and Date | Briefing of Plot | Attitude | Word Recognition | Skills Needed |
|---|---|---|---|---|
| 2/3 King Arthur | Style too difficult but there is definitely some comprehension | Because he's reading —got books for Xmas King Arthur 3 Musketeers Treasure Island | an on/anon parten/partner | Uses context clues— VOWELS i short sounds |
| 2/13 Two Is a Team | Read to class | Likes to be read to. Hard books are frustrating. Speak to mother about this. | | Vowels— double vowels syllables |
| 3/24 King Arthur | OK gets most words part of meaning | Returned to book—couldn't put it down. Read books in between | groving/groveling | Same |

Name  Barry C.[3]

| | | | | |
|---|---|---|---|---|
| 12/1 Cowboy Sam Experience Stories | Can't do it. | | he/here<br>horse<br>hat | Sight vocabulary<br>Initial consonants |
| 1/28 Cowboy Sam | Book is now memorized | Continues to read, re-read, and draw pictures from it. | find<br>water<br>to/for<br>went/was<br>cattle/cow<br>can't/could | Experience stories sight vocab. readiness activities require reading other primers |
| 2/14 Tuffy and Boots | Can recognize characters in pictures | Has reached a sense of accomplishment | likes/wants<br>we/he | sight vocabulary |
| 5/21 Mr. and Mrs. Big | OK | The return of reading —will wonders ever cease! | | Will he continue? |
| Roger D. | | | | |
| 10/15 Blazer the Gypsies | Needs help to recall parts, but has general idea. However, read pictures not the text. | Reads comic books "more fun reading whole books" | gypsy<br>took/tried (repeated)<br>house/horse<br>would<br>short/suddenly<br>sailed | b d reversal<br>work on picture clues and context clues |

[1] Records by Marilyn Zucker, 4th grade, Farmingdale, New York.
[2] Word as said/actual word.
[3] As of 12/2 Nonreader in 4th grade.

## Book Lists and Where You Can Find Them

American Literary Association, 50 E. Huron St., Chicago 11, Ill.
—see: "The Booklist and Subscription Books Bulletin." Published biweekly with children's book section; also: A Basic Book Collection for Elementary Grades, 1956.

Association for Childhood Education International, 1200 Fifteenth St., N.W., Washington 5, D.C.—Monthly children's book section in "Childhood Education." Yearly book lists and occasional other bibliographies.

R. R. Bowker and Co., 62 W. 45th St., New York 35, N. Y.
—"Growing Up With Books" lists and "Junior Libraries" magazine with monthly children's book section.

"Bulletin of the Center for Children's Books," University of Chicago Press, 5750 Ellis Ave., Chicago 37, Ill.—Published 11 months a year with critical evaluation of each book including reading level and books *not* recommended.

Bureau of Educational Research, Board of Education of City of New York, 110 Livingston St., Brooklyn 1, N. Y.—"Books for Individualized Reading—For the Beginning Reader"; "Books for Individualized Reading—For the Children Who Are Beginning to Gain Independence in Reading."

Educational Clinic, "High Interest—Low Vocabulary Booklist," Boston University School of Education, 332 Bay State Road, Boston 15, Mass.

Horn Book, 264 Boylston St., Boston, Mass.—an illustrated journal about children's books, authors and artists in six issues annually.

Junior Reviewers, Box 36, Aspen, Colorado.—Published bimonthly —unique feature of each book reviewed twice, once by a child, once by an adult.

Larrick, Nancy, *Parent's Guide to Children's Reading,* Pocket Books (Mail Service Dept., 630 Fifth Avenue, New York 20, N. Y., 35¢ plus 5¢ postage), Chaps. 18, 19, 20.

Major newspapers with Sunday magazine sections, such as New York Times. (Check those available to you locally.)—a children's book supplement around Christmas and/or Book Week.

National Council of Teachers of English, 704 S. Sixth St., Champaign, Ill.

*Elementary English,* monthly children's book review section, 1956 list.

Saturday Review of Literature, 25 W. 45th St., New York 36, N. Y.—reviews children's books four times a year.

Strang, R., Gilbert, C., and Scoggio, M. C., *Gateways to Readable Books* (2nd ed.), New York City: H. W. Wilson, 1952.—for middle and upper grades.

In your own library—Children's Catalog published by H. W. Wilson Co.—Published every five years with yearly supplements.

## Additional References Relating to Individualized Reading

Blake, H. E., Bucklin, B. M., and Knoll, M., "Here's Another Way," National Council of Teachers of English. Portfolio *Creative Ways in Teaching the Language Arts* 1957.

Boney, C. DeWitt, *A Study of Library Reading in the Primary Grades.* Contributions to Education, No. 578. New York: Teachers College, Columbia U., 1933.

Brogan, Peggy, and Fox, Lorene, *"Helping Children Learn."* Yonkers-on-Hudson: World Book, 1955, pp. 104-10.

Bureau of Educational Research, Wrightstone, J. W., Director, and Lazar, May, Assistant Director. Board of Education of the City of New York. Mimeographed material.

—*Thinking About Individualized Reading,* April 1956, reprinted January 1957.

—*Vocabulary Study,* January 1957.

—*Interim Report—Survey in Selected Schools 1956-57,* June 1957.

—*Books for Individualized Reading—For the Beginning Reader* (Grades 1-2), October 1957.

—*Books for Individualized Reading—For the Children* (Grades 2-3) *Who Are Beginning to Gain Independence in Reading,* October 1957.

—*Individualized Reading and the Reading Skills,* January 1958.

—*Effective Classroom Practices in Individualized Reading,* May 1958.

—*Problems in Individualized Reading,* August 1958.

Burrows, Alvina T., "Individualizing the Teaching of Reading." Ch. X, *Teaching Children in the Middle Grades*. Boston: D. C. Heath, 1952.

———, "Caste System or Democracy" *Elementary English*, March 1950, pp. 145-7. Vol. XXVII.

Butler, Elsie, "Experiences in Third Grade," *Elementary English*, February 1951.

Carr, Constance, *Individualizing Development of Abilities and Skills in Reading: A Description and Critique of an Emerging Practice*. Unpublished doctoral dissertation, Teachers College, Columbia University, 1958.

√Carson, Louise G., "Moving Towards Individualization." *Elementary English*, October 1957.

Cole, Mildred, "Teaching Reading Where There Are Varying Abilities" *Grade Teacher* Vol. 68, p. 31, April 1951.

Coryell, Nancy G., *An Evaluation of Intensive and Extensive Teaching of Literature*. New York City, Bureau of Publications, Teachers College, Columbia University.

Dean, Ray B., "A Plan for Individual Reading in the Intermediate Grades." *National Elementary Principal,* 17:557-63 July 1938.

Duker, Sam, "Research Report" *Reading in Action*. 1957 Proceedings of International Reading Association, p. 60.

Durin, Margaret, "One Way to Meet Individual Differences." *National Elementary Principal,* September 1955.

√Evans, N. Dean, "An Individualized Reading Program for the Elementary Teacher." *Elementary English,* May, 1953.

Field, Helen A., *Extensive Individual Reading vs. Class Reading,* New York City, Teachers College, Columbia University, 1930, 52 pp.

Garretson, Grace; Whitcomb, Irene, and Termeer, Beatrice, "Through Self-Selection—Progress Unlimited." Bulletin #98, *Reading,* Association for Childhood Education International, 1956.

Gurney, Tess, "My Individualized Reading Program." *Childhood Education,* March 1956.

Harris, Albert J., *How to Increase Reading Ability*. New York City: Longmans, Green and Co. 1957 (3rd Edition) p. 115f.

Hester, Kathleen, "Every Child Reads Successfully in Multiple Level Program." *Elementary School Journal,* October 1952.

* Hildreth, Gertrude *Teaching Reading.* New York City: Henry Holt 1958, pp. 29-31, 257, 418-19, 416.

Hosking, Elizabeth, *A Study of Children's Voluntary Reading.* Unpublished M.A. thesis. Ann Arbor: U. of Michigan, University Elementary School, 1938.

Hurley, Beatrice, *Curriculum for Elementary School Children.* New York City: Ronald Press, 1957, pp. 169-174, 207-212.

Jacobs, Leland B., "Reading on Their Own Means Reading at Their Growing Edges." *Reading Teacher,* Vol. 6, No. 4, pp. 27-32, March 1953.

Jenkins, Marian, et al., "Here's to Success in Reading." *Childhood Education,* November 1954, pp. 124-128.

Johnson, Eleanor, *Individualizing Reading.* Curriculum Letter #35, Middletown, Conn. Wesleyan University, March 1957.

Jones, Daisy M., "An Experiment in Adaptation to Individual Differences." *Journal of Educational Psychology,* 39: 257-272, 1948.

Kaar, Harold, "An Experiment With an Individualized Method of Teaching Reading." *The Reading Teacher,* Vol. 7, No. 3, pp. 174-177. February 1954.

Kingsley, Marjorie, "An Experiment in Individualized Reading." Elementary English, February, 1958.

LaBrant, Lon, and Heller, Frieda. *An Evaluation of Free Reading in Grades 7-12.* The State University School, Columbus, 1939. #4 Ohio Contributions to Education.

Lazar, May, "Individualized Reading: A Dynamic Approach." *The Reading Teacher,* December 1957, p. 75f.

LeBaron, Walter, "Some Practical Suggestions in Developing a Program of Continuous Progress." *Elementary School Journal,* Vol. 46, October 1945, pp. 84-9.

Lee, J. Murray, "Individualized Instruction." *Education,* January 1954, p. 279f.

Miel, Alice (editor), *Individualizing Reading Practices.* New York: Bureau of Publications, Teachers College, Columbia University, 1958 #14 Practical Suggestions for Teacher Series.

Olson, Willard C., and Davis, Sarita I., "The Adaptation of Instruction in Reading to the Growth of Children." *Educational Method* 20: 71-79, 1940.

National Council of Teachers of English, "Reading," Chapter VI, in *Language Arts for Today's Children*. New York: Appleton-Century-Crofts, Inc. 1954, pp. 144-205.

Palmer, Delores C., *To Determine the Reaction of a Fourth Grade to a Program of Self Selection of Reading Materials*. Unpublished M.A. Thesis, University of Utah, Salt Lake City. *See also* Chapter VI, Hughes, Marie, "Theoretical Considerations Underlying Program of Self-Selection with Recommendations."

Robinson, Helen, "What Research Says to the Teacher of Reading." *Reading Teacher*, February 1955, p. 173f.

Rowe, R. and Dornhoefer, E., "Individualized Reading." *Childhood Education*, Vol. 34 #3 pp. 118-20, November 1957.

Wenzel, Evelyn, "Guidance in Independent Reading." *Reading Teacher*, Vol. 9 #3, February 1956.

Wollner, Mary H., *Voluntary Reading as an Expression of Individuality*. Contributions to Education, No. 944, New York: Teachers College, Columbia U., 1949.

Worlton, J. T., "Individualizing Instruction in Reading" *Elementary School Journal*, Vol. XXXVIII, September 1936, pp. 735-47.

Young, Marion, "A Report on Self-Selection in Reading." *Elementary English*, March 1958, p. 176.

Zirbes, Laura, *Individualized Reading*. Schoolmen's Week Proceedings, Philadelphia, Pennsylvania, University of Pennsylvania, 1951.

————, *Practice Exercises and Checks on Silent Reading in the Primary Grades. Report of Experimentation*. Lincoln School of Teachers College, Columbia University, 1925.